THE FALKLANDS CONFLICT

On 19 March, 1982 a party of Argentine
demolition workers landed at Leith Harbour,
South Georgia, with a contract to dismantle the
island's long-abandoned whaling station. The
contract was *bona fide* but the landing was in open
defiance of all British customs and
requirements. When the
settlement at Grytvi
obtain a visa o
ran up the Arg
Argentine troop   Falkland
Islands.

Thus was launched   alklands conflict. An
international crisis of major proportions loomed
threateningly over the horizon and in Britain an
affair that had begun for most people as a small
item at the end of a workaday news summary
suddenly became more than mere headlines – the
world watched aghast as Britain prepared for war.

Now, for the first time, Dobson, Miller and Payne
tell the full story: the launch of the British task
force, the ultimate failure of the United Nations to
find a peaceful solution acceptable to both sides
and the long, campaign in the South Atlantic.

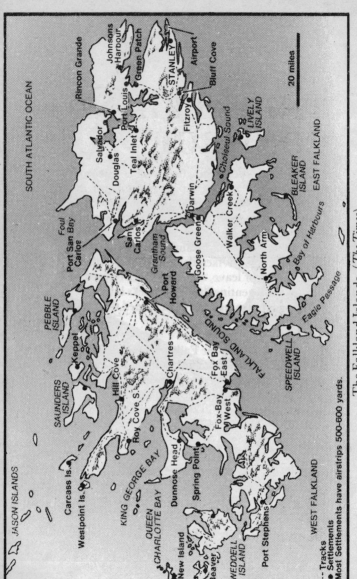

The Falkland Islands. (*The Times*)

THE FALKLANDS CONFLICT

**Christopher Dobson
John Miller
Ronald Payne**

CORONET BOOKS
Hodder and Stoughton

Copyright © 1982 by Christopher Dobson,
John Miller, Ronald Payne

First published in Great Britain 1982 by Coronet Books

The authors would like to thank Kenneth Clarke for his advice and
research from Buenos Aires and the Falkland Islands

British Library C.I.P.

Dobson, Christopher
   The Falklands Conflict.
   1. Falkland Islands – Politics and Government
   1. Title   2. Miller, John
   3. Payne, Ronald
   997'. II   F3031

ISBN 0-340-32408-2

This book is sold subject to the condition that
it shall not, by way of trade or otherwise, be
lent, re-sold, hired out or otherwise circulated
without the publisher's prior consent in any
form of binding or cover other than that in
which this is published and without a similar
condition including this condition being
imposed on the subsequent purchaser.

Printed and bound in Great Britain for
Hodder and Stoughton Paperbacks, a
division of Hodder and Stoughton Ltd.,
Mill Road, Dunton Green, Sevenoaks,
Kent (Editorial Office: 47 Bedford
Square, London, WC1 3DP) by
Cox and Wyman Ltd., Reading.
Photoset by Rowland Phototypesetting Ltd.,
Bury St Edmunds, Suffolk.

Argentina and the Falkland Islands. (*Daily Telegraph*)

THE FALKLAN

ARGENTINA

3 A-69 corvettes

4 diesel-powered submarines

2 Type 42 destroyers

1 aircraft carrier (The 25th of May)

2 Fletcher Type destroyers

1 cruiser (General Belgrano)

1 Gearing Type destroyer

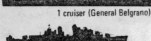

3 Sumner Type destroyers

9 Canberra long-range bombers

10 Dassault-Breguet Super Etendard carrier-based attack aircraft

25 armed helicopters

43 Mirage fighters

68 Skyhawk bombers

14 light helicopters

𝟆 𝟆 𝟆 𝟆 𝟆 𝟆 𝟆
𝟆 𝟆 𝟆 𝟆 𝟆 𝟆 𝟆
𝟆 𝟆 𝟆 𝟆 𝟆 𝟆 𝟆
10,000 troops on Falkland Islands (plus tanks, armoured cars, mortar emplacements and shore batteries)

1,000 troops on South Georgia

𝟆 𝟆 𝟆

Not illustrated:
150,000 troops on mainland

THE FORCES ASSEMBLED: HOW IT LOOKED AT THE BEGINNING

Artwork courtesy of H. Bunch Associates Ltd.

DS CONFLICT
BRITAIN

32 Sea Harrier VTOL
strike planes

2 Type 22 destroyers

4 nuclear submarines

2 aircraft carriers
(Hermes and Invincible)

Lynx helicopters

3 Nimrod early
warning planes

3 Type 42 destroyers

2 Type 12 frigates

2 County class destroyers

3 Type 21 frigates

2 assault ships

5,000 marines
(estimated total, exact
figure military secret)

Additional ships
not illustrated:

Royal Fleet Auxiliaries:
4 tankers
2 fleet replenishment
ships
1 stores support ship
5 landing and logistics
ships

Civil ships:
2 troop/hospital ships
(Canberra and Uganda)
2 roll-on, roll-off ships
1 maintenance ship
1 freshwater ship
3 salvage tugs
4 deep water trawlers
(used as minesweepers)
10 tankers

18 Sea King
helicopters

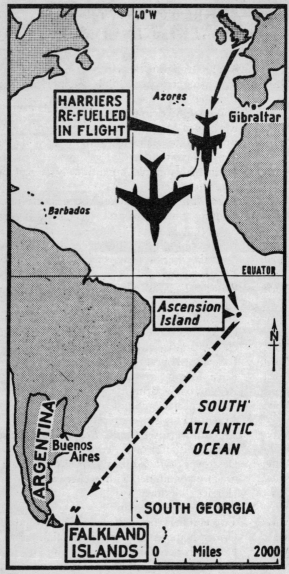

The strategic importance of Ascension Island to the British. (*Daily Telegraph*)

A CHRONOLOGY OF THE
1982 FALKLANDS CONFLICT

26 Feb:	Anglo-Argentine talks in New York
19 March:	Argentine scrap merchants land at Leith, South Georgia
22 March:	Foreign Office says landing was illegal
27 March:	Reports of Argentine naval movements
29 March:	Britain states its concern about a "potentially dangerous situation"
1 April:	Prime Minister told Argentine invasion of Falklands imminent
2 April:	Argentina invades. Royal Marines surrender
3 April:	Commons meets for first weekend sitting since Suez, 1956
	UN Resolution calls for Argentine withdrawal
5 April:	Lord Carrington resigns as Foreign Secretary. Task force sails
7 April:	Britain declares 200-mile war zone around Falklands
9 April:	Haig assumes mediation role
10 April:	EEC backs trade sanctions against Argentina
17 April:	Haig has talks with Argentine military junta
19 April:	Haig shuttle breaks down
25 April:	Royal Marines recapture South Georgia
30 April:	Reagan backs Britain
1 May:	Vulcan attack on Stanley airport
	Argentina loses two aircraft
2 May:	Argentine cruiser *General Belgrano* sunk by submarine with loss of 301 crew
4 May:	Destroyer *Sheffield* hit by Exocet missile, set on fire and abandoned with twenty lives lost
	Harrier shot down
5 May:	Peru drafts peace plan
6 May:	Two Harriers lost, believed to have collided
7 May:	United Nations enter peace negotiations
9 May:	Falklands bombarded from sea and air
11 May:	Argentine supply ship sunk
12 May:	Three Argentine Skyhawks brought down

14 May:	Prime Minister warns that peaceful settlement may not be possible
15 May:	Marines land on Pebble Island, destroy eleven Argentine aircraft, and withdraw
17 May:	Peace talks continue at UN as Mrs Thatcher speaks of "one last go"
19 May:	UN peace initiative effectively collapses
20 May:	Mrs Thatcher accuses Argentina of "obduracy and delay, deception and bad faith"
	British task force ordered into battle
21 May:	Force of 5,000 British troops establish bridge-head at San Carlos
	The frigate HMS *Ardent* sunk by air attack in Falkland Sound
	Seventeen Argentine aircraft shot down by fleet
22 May:	Consolidation day at bridgehead
23 May:	Argentine Air Force returns
	The frigate HMS *Antelope* hit and damaged
	Seven Argentine aircraft shot down
24 May:	HMS *Antelope* sinks after unexploded bomb detonates
	Eight Argentine planes shot down
25 May:	Argentine National Day. Destroyer HMS *Coventry* sunk by Skyhawk bombers after shooting down five Argentine aircraft
	Atlantic Conveyor abandoned having been hit by Exocet missile
27 May:	Darwin and Goose Green fall to 2nd Battalion, the Parachute Regiment. 250 Argentines soldiers killed and 1,400 captured. 17 British soldiers killed
	Royal Marines capture Douglas and Teal Inlet
29 May:	Warships and Harriers bombard Stanley
30 May:	Shelling continues as British troops advance
31 May:	Mount Kent taken by British troops
4 June:	Britain vetoes Panamanian–Spanish ceasefire resolution in the UN Security Council

INTRODUCTION

When, on 2 April, 1982 the first soldiers of the Argentine special forces landed at Stanley and opened fire, they began a process which will go down in history as the conflict which need never have happened. With more foresight, with greater understanding of the forces at work in the South Atlantic and, in particular the bizarre behaviour of the Argentine junta, the British government could have prevented the landing from ever taking place.

Even in the heyday of British imperial power and wealth, the natural caution of Prime Ministers and of the Treasury had always prevented the use of great military resources in protecting outlying segments of empire. Parsimony has always been the tradition of British military activity and with foresight and meanness the defence of faraway places was usually left to a couple of frigates and a battalion of troops at the most.

Had such a force been alerted the moment that threats to the Falkland Islands became detectable, it could have posed such a threat to Argentine invasion forces as to prevent them from seizing what had once been known as Fortress Falklands. But the successful use of military resources limited by economic pressures depends upon the excellence of information provided by the intelligence services and by the Foreign Office. Advance warning of hostile moves needs to be assessed correctly and acted upon with anticipatory speed by government. Yet while the Argentines were manoeuvring their scrap dealer vanguard of invasion in South Georgia and hoisting the Argentine flag there, little was done. The only response was the belated dispatch of Lieutenant Mills and his twenty-one Royal Marine Commandos in the ice patrol ship HMS *Endurance*.

The Falkland Islands themselves were defended only by a small force of Marines some eighty strong. That was more than usual because the detachment already there on a year's tour of duty was to be relieved in April by a new platoon of forty men. In a pointless attempt to save the Argentines from irritation, officials in London stressed that there was no increase in the force and that more men were present only because of the normal change-over. As it turned out, the replacement unit had arrived at a convenient time and in the circumstances both units were ordered to stay on, for by this time the original small garrison was below strength.

Another handicap was that the relieving Marines had arrived without their weapons. They flew in by way of Montevideo in Uruguay and, as was customary in such transits, they arrived in civilian clothes. The result was that when they were most needed, more than half of the defending force had not brought along its own automatic weapons, machine guns and rocket launchers. The intention had been for the new unit to take over arms and stores from the unit it relieved, but the *Endurance* detachment had already sailed with their weapons to South Georgia.

When the moment came for the Marines to put up at least a token resistance to the helicopter-borne Argentine special forces, many of them had found it necessary to borrow weapons and ammunition stored by the local home guards. The Falklands Defence Force, a group of part-time soldiers who did a little training each year, fortunately had its own armoury of weapons and ammunition of the same types as those used by the regulars. But the result was that even an experienced unit on the spot had to mount a makeshift defence without the benefit of mines or other equipment, and without even a proper stock of barbed wire.

This was the force required to stand up to the first shock of invasion by 150 soldiers from crack Argentine units, followed by a further 2,000 men who landed in amphibious armoured personnel carriers from a powerful Argentine task force offshore. The flagship of the fleet was the carrier *Veinticinco de Mayo* and it had eight other warships in attendance.

The small British force on the island was meant to act as a trip wire of warning to the aggressor. Sir Michael Hadow, a former British ambassador to Argentina, recalled that he had occasion to warn the then government in Buenos Aires that if so much as one Marine were killed in the Falklands, then a state of war would exist. But on this occasion there was little point in standing by such a warning, for even if there had been casualties, there was no help at hand from the Royal Navy. The only warship in the area was the ice-patrol ship, mother ship of the Antarctic Survey, the *Endurance*. Rumours were put about that nuclear submarines were heading for the South Atlantic but these have never been substantiated. Nor could the Royal Air Force help. Without tanker refuelling aircraft in position transport planes could not get there in time, and because the air strip at Stanley was too short there was no question of using long-range big jets to fly in reinforcements. That was the fault of previous governments which had never been prepared to pay out an extra 5 million pounds to construct a full-length runway.

To blame the government of Mrs Margaret Thatcher for giving President Galtieri the chance to seize the Falkland Islands so painlessly is not to exculpate earlier governments of both parties for their share of guilt in what happened in April 1982. The islands were unloved, neglected and starved of help. Successive administrations had done little to discourage the belief in Buenos Aires that at some point they would be allowed to become masters of the *Malvinas*.

The problem of the future of the Falklands and of Argentina's emotional claims to their possession was not a new one, but it was a question to which neither governments, nor public opinion, nor the media had paid great attention. An opinion poll revealed that a large number of Britons thought that the Falklands were somewhere off the coast of Scotland. An article in *The Times* a few days before the invasion was headlined "These paltry islands which separate us", the "us" referring to Britain and Argentina. The Falklands were no more than a tiresome worry easily swallowed up and forgotten in the sea of troubles which surrounded Britain in the 1980s.

Nevertheless within a week of the assault, the accusation was made by Mr James Callaghan, a former Labour Prime Minister, that Mrs Thatcher had blundered in failing to anticipate the invasion. The Shadow Foreign Secretary, Denis Healey, followed up by declaring that the Prime Minister had no moral or political right to ask the Opposition for a blank cheque of support after so monumental a lack of judgment.

It was left to Dr David Owen, the Social Democratic Party spokesman, to demand a full enquiry into the conduct of the whole affair. He was well placed to do so, for while Foreign Secretary in the Labour government of 1977 he had dispatched a modest Royal Navy force to the South Atlantic to ward off Argentine threats to the Falklands. Mrs Thatcher assured him that such an enquiry would be carried out in due course. Dr Owen has revealed to the authors of this book details of the steps which had been taken in 1977 to ward off threats of an Argentine invasion. "There is without doubt a certain parallelism between what happened then and what happened more recently," he said. "On that occasion we made a contingency arrangement to call the Argentines' bluff. I persuaded the Cabinet Defence and Overseas Policy Committee to order the nuclear submarine HMS *Dreadnought* to sail from Gibraltar for the South Atlantic in November, 1977. The Navy insisted that for reasons of communication she had to be accompanied by two warships. The frigates HMS *Phoebe* and *Alacrity* also sailed, together with two Royal Fleet Auxiliary vessels. This operation was conducted in secrecy because the aim was to have them in position to buttress diplomacy. Had it become necessary, the Argentine government could have been informed of their presence in the area with orders to open fire should Argentine ships attempt an invasion. At the time we did not even tell the Americans the purpose of the force, simply informing them of naval exercises in the South Atlantic."

On that occasion diplomacy, backed by a small fleet, was enough to dissuade the Argentines from taking action. In 1982 Mrs Thatcher's government failed to take comparable steps. The critical time came late in February when talks were held in New York between Foreign Office minister Mr Luce, the Argentines and representatives of the Falkland Islanders. Although Mr Luce had the impression that all was going well, press reports from Buenos Aires were already hinting at invasion threats. It was a critical moment because the Royal Navy had estimated that it needed twenty-six sailing days to place a preventive task force in the area. Dr Owen, an expert witness in such matters, believes that it would still have been possible to dispatch a nuclear-powered submarine to the area so that, at the "first whiff of invasion", the United States could have been told a submarine was on station with orders to open fire with its conventional weapons, should it be necessary. The United States, which is always aware of submarine movements, could then have informed the Argentine government of her presence and orders. He believes that such a warning might have been sufficient to prevent the attack.

By the time the government did hint that the submarine HMS *Superb* was in the area it was too late to affect Argentine plans. In any case the rumours of her movements did not carry the same weight they would have done if the Americans had confirmed to Buenos Aires that she was on station.

With hindsight it can now be seen that two moves by the British government were interpreted by the Argentines to mean that there was no disposition in London to hold on to the Falkland Islands. Mr Nicholas Ridley, a Foreign Office minister, had raised with the islanders the idea of 'lease-back', namely that Britain should lease the islands from the Argentine government. The islanders disliked the proposal intensely. In June of 1981 it was announced that HMS *Endurance*, the ice-patrol ship and sole Royal Navy vessel permanently stationed in the South Atlantic, would be withdrawn.

Dr David Owen wrote a letter to the Foreign Secretary

protesting against this decision. He believed it would convince the Argentines that Britain was losing interest in the islands. Significantly it was Mr John Nott, the Defence Secretary who eventually replied on 15 January, 1982: "The decision to pay her off was by no means easy, but let me try to put that decision into context . . . Against the background of the decisions I announced then (the July 81 Defence White Paper), I had reluctantly to conclude that the relatively limited contribution made by HMS *Endurance* (which, as you may recall, is equipped with two 20mm Oerlikon guns and carries two Wasp helicopters) to our defence capability did not justify the continued expense of running her. She will accordingly be withdrawn from service when she returns to the United Kingdom next spring. Royal Navy ships will, however, continue to deploy to the South Atlantic from time to time though obviously less frequently than HMS *Endurance* has been able to do."

The Defence Secretary went on to insist that the government had no doubt about British sovereignty over the Falklands and would defend them. But his tone gave the impression that it was the need to save money and to concentrate on having a NATO Navy which was paramount. As for Dr Owen, he concluded that this judgment of priorities should have been a matter for Lord Carrington who, if there had been proper consultation, should have overruled Defence Ministry decisions on a matter of such importance to the Falklands.

Although there was no disposition to conduct any hasty investigation, while the fate of the Falklands was being decided in battle, the question of responsibility must now be faced. How did it come about that the British government, indeed the nation, was taken so much off guard and at a disadvantage on British territory by the military actions of a third rank power such as Argentina?

The first scapegoat for the disaster was inevitably the Foreign Office, whose duty it is to safeguard British interests overseas. Indeed the Foreign Secretary, Lord Carrington resigned and took two junior ministers with him. But the

Foreign Office is only one of the organs of state responsible for gathering, processing and assessing reports on the intentions, warlike or otherwise, of foreign governments. Final decisions based upon that information are in the hands of the Cabinet and ultimately the Prime Minister.

There can have been no secret about the fact that Argentina was building up her naval power: she had purchased warships, including two modern destroyers, and electronic weapons from Britain. Royal Navy officers had given instruction to Argentine sailors. It should have been obvious that the junta had its own good reasons for spending money on naval refurbishment.

The Argentine naval attaché in London, himself a Marine, visited the Ministry of Defence and, at his request, also visited the Royal Marines training establishment at Lympstone in Devon. Soldiers of the Argentine special forces had attended training courses with the crack British unit skilled in subversive warfare, the Special Air Service. There is some reason to believe, as we shall show, that some of them put their British instruction to good use with the special forces of Argentina in the original landings at Stanley. Only a few months before the invasion an Argentine diplomat had bought a considerable quantity of charts of the Falkland Islands from a London map dealer. Here already was a local indication, for those with eyes to see, that the Argentines were taking special interest in the Falkland Islands.

The coordinating agency which supplies the Defence and Overseas Cabinet Committee with intelligence summaries is the Joint Intelligence Committee, presided over by Sir Antony Acland when the crisis began. But in April he was promoted to be head of the diplomatic service, replacing Sir Michael Palliser whose long-planned retirement upon reaching the upper age limit then took place. The new chief of the Joint Committee is Mr Patrick Wright, upon whom will eventually fall the task of assessing to what extent the intelligence agencies were to blame for the Falklands disaster. It is customary for the Joint Committee to be under Foreign Office chairmanship, while among its members are representatives of the Secret Intelligence Service, of MI5, the Home Office, and the Defence Ministry. There are no political ministers on this Committee and the Committee draws its information together from many sources.

Photographic material garnered by United States satellites is made available to the British from the Reconnaissance Office in Washington under special relationship arrangements. American satellites were surveying the area when the Argentine fleet was preparing for sea, and the Joint Committee must have been aware of naval movements. Perhaps even more important was the signals intelligence obtained from the long-range eavesdropping of communications traffic both military and governmental. Ascension Island has a powerful station for carrying out such electronic espionage. In return for the use of the British island, the American National Security Agency pools information obtained with the British government.

It must be assumed that a certain amount of top secret Argentine traffic was passed in computer-based codes which may not have been cracked. But Mr Ted Rowlands, a Labour MP who was formerly a junior minister dealing with the Falklands up to 1979, tactlessly told the House of Commons that British code breakers had little difficulty in unscrambling secret Argentine messages.

Apart from technological sources of information, the Joint Committee in London has at its disposal regular diplomatic reports from such embassies as that in Buenos Aires. Some of these reports come from Defence Attachés abroad who are also in touch with their own ministry. Finally, the Secret Intelligence Service has its own covert sources within Argentina. After the invasion, the *Daily Telegraph* correspondent in Buenos Aires was told by an "impeccable" intelligence source that strong warnings of impending action had been going out to the British from Argentina.

In addition to all these lines of information stretching out from London, the chiefs of staff at the Defence Ministry have their own inflow of military intelligence. Their information committee is also in touch with the Joint Committee.

With such a network of intelligence gathering at its disposal it appears scarcely credible that the Joint Committee could have been taken completely by surprise by the Argentine moves. There must be a strong presumption, if the government *was* taken by surprise, that its members failed to digest the quantity of raw material effectively enough or fast enough to pass on summaries to the decision-making political ministers. It is also possible that not enough attention was paid to sorting the wheat from the mass of chaff.

It is at this level that the responsibility of the Foreign Office is engaged. Great weight would be attached to the judgments of the Latin American desk of the FO on the Falklands affair. Did the Foreign Office override the importance of the signals coming in about activity in the South Atlantic with its own understanding of the junta's intentions, arrived at from its own diplomatic readings? Or, was it a question of ministers and officials being too busy with what were considered at the time to be more important matters such as the Middle East, Poland and the affairs of the European Community? Lord Carrington was travelling a good deal, and from his experience in charge of the Foreign Office, Dr David Owen asserts that unless the minister is constantly on the spot in Whitehall it is extremely difficult to keep tight control over all foreign affairs. Another disadvantage for Lord Carrington was that he sat not in the House of Commons, but in the House of Lords, where he was less subject to the day to day probing and influence of MPs.

It is likely that the operations of the Argentine Navy were known in London on 26 March. Lord Carrington himself admitted that ministers were aware of these developments, but according to him the Buenos Aires junta had not yet taken the final decision to invade. Not unless official papers are made available in a full scale investigation shall we know for certain what transpired at that crucial time, whether officials blundered in their summaries, or whether harassed ministers simply scribbled on their papers, "No Action". It must be stressed that the Prime Minister, Mrs Thatcher, herself receives daily intelligence and Foreign Office assessments.

If it is assumed that the Cabinet had some awareness of the threats from Argentina, it seems incredible that they were so relaxed at the time. But Mrs Thatcher's government, well aware how many times wolf had been cried, was not convinced of the urgent need to mount a costly expedition to protect islands they did not then hold dear, in order to ward off a threat which might come to nothing. This explanation is especially likely when the government was intent on making every possible economy in order to demonstrate how well its monetary policy was succeeding. An important clue was given by Lord Carrington, interviewed on TV after his resignation, when he said: ". . . the assessments were different". Then he added, "Well, what we got wrong was that the Argentines invaded . . ." This gave the clear impression that there were different schools of thought and the government got it wrong by believing that there would be no invasion.

The joker in the pack of cards held by the intelligence assessors was the President of Argentina, General Galtieri himself. He had prepared the way for seizing power by making a pilgrimage to Washington in August '81, and there he made a certain impression on some members of the Reagan administration. He had talked about hemispheric cooperation, he had mentioned the idea of a South Atlantic Treaty Organisation, to keep out the Soviet Union, linking pro-western Latin American states with the US and possibly with South Africa. All that sounded welcome to American ears.

In December, President Galtieri ousted the former President and emerged at the apex of the officers' triumvirate which controlled Argentina. He offered assistance to President Reagan in El Salvador and he cultivated the friendship of Vernon Walters, a former Deputy Director of the CIA, who was responsible for developing contacts in Buenos Aires and trouble-shooting in Latin America. After the invasion Mr Walters declared, "It's a silly war." He also said, "What you really have here is a problem of two machismos, and the

machismo of women is even more sensitive than the machismo of men."

The new President of Argentina had begun to purge
some of the most notorious officers who had conducted such
zealous and brutal operations against Argentine terrorists.
He wanted to show that he realised how their actions had
offended American opinion by their aggressive disregard of
human rights. The President was trying to make Argentina a
respectable ally of the United States, and somehow he seems
to have got the impression that in return the Americans
might look sympathetically on Argentine claims to the Falklands. To acquire the Falklands was a venerable ambition
and President Galtieri wanted to fulfil it before the 150th
anniversary of the British 'occupation' in 1984.

But President Galtieri was by no means the all-powerful
dictator. Not only were there the checks and balances of the
military constitution upon him, but also threats to his power
from his envious and ambitious Air Force and Navy colleagues in the three officer junta. It was the divisions and
quarrels within that junta which made the task so difficult for
those trying to assess its aims and likely policy decisions. The
ruling officers were, in the words of Mr Alexander Haig, "a
bunch of thugs", perpetually disputing among themselves,
as all the would-be mediators subsequently discovered.

Admiral Jorge Isaac Anaya, who represented the Argentine Navy on the junta, was the most aggressive advocate of
seizing the Falklands. It was he who set up the South Georgia
flag-raising incident by the scrap men, which provided the
pretext for action. Together with his naval cronies he had
refurbished the contingency plan for the whole operation,
possibly without the knowledge of President Galtieri who at
that time was hard-pressed with the desperately ailing economy and with the threat of street rioting by Peronist supporters. It is now known that later in mid-April, and on his own
initiative, Admiral Anaya ordered his only aircraft carrier to
sea without telling fellow members of the junta. The timing of
the operation reinforces the belief that he was then in the
ascendant.

On 29 March, the Argentine fleet was reported to be sailing for joint exercises with the Uruguayan Navy, and British intelligence was aware of this. Daily reports of fleet movements were available in London, where it was still believed that this was a routine naval exercise. Not until 31 March, only two days before the invasion, did it become known for certain to the British that the Argentine fleet had broken off from the exercises and was sailing at speed towards the Falklands. Yet it was not until the following day, Thursday, 1 April, in the afternoon, that the Foreign Office warned Mr Rex Hunt, Governor of the Falklands, that an invasion was expected at dawn next day. Until then, all that had been predicted was the arrival of a landing party from a submarine.

It looks very much as though Admiral Anaya, having hatched his plot quietly, began executing the final man-oeuvre after the 30 March mass rally of labour Peronist protesters in Buenos Aires. This rally was almost out of hand until security forces, armed with tear gas, moved in to make mass arrests. That near-riot alarmed the junta and finally convinced President Galtieri (who by then feared that even his Presidency was in danger) to give full support to the Admiral's plan. There could be no surer way of pleasing and uniting the country behind him than by capturing the Falkland Islands.

The conflict had begun. London knew it was too late for military or naval action to forestall the invasion. If Mrs Thatcher, conferring with her ministers and admirals that Wednesday evening in Downing Street, was shocked and surprised, then President Galtieri, Admiral Anaya and their air force colleague General Lami Dozo were soon to be completely astounded by the strength of the reaction from London which they had totally misjudged.

THE HISTORY OF THE CONFLICT

Most maps of the world show the Falkland Islands as tiny pink dots way down in the blue South Atlantic hard by sprawling Argentina. Stanley is the capital with a population so tiny as to be often omitted altogether, but a (*Br*) makes it clear who owns the dots.

This is not the case if you buy your map in Argentina, or in some other countries in South America. The islands are still 300 miles east of the Patagonian coastline but on Latin American maps they have a different name – *Islas Malvinas* – and an (*Ar*).

Over the years the Falklanders had learned to live with this conflict of interests: as far as they were concerned they were British and that was the end of it. More British, perhaps, than the British. After all, the islands had been settled by Britain for some 150 years and the 2,000 or so inhabitants, many of whom were descendants of Scots and English and Welsh shepherds, were all extremely loyal to the crown.

Why would Argentina want to "repossess" the islands in any case? What was so special about the two main islands, East Falkland and West Falkland, and the 200 islets which surround them? They are rainswept: on average rain falls for 200 days each year. Their 4,700 square miles make them less than half the size of Wales. Peat-bog and fells dominate the landscape, some of whose place names convey the inhospitable scenery – Mount Misery, No Man's Land and Tumbledown Mountain.

Perhaps it was the 658,000 sheep, or the several million penguins, or the kelp geese or the king shags that attracted the Argentines. Or the three shack pubs in Stanley (popula-

tion 1,050 in 1980) or the three churches, or the maroon
London taxicab which was the flagship of the Governor, or
the Tennants canned beer, or the Smarties, or the endless
meals of fishfingers and braised, grilled, hamburgered or
cold lamb? Or perhaps it was the talk – and that is all it has
been up to now – of a potential offshore oil bonanza.

In fact at the very heart of the Falkland crisis is the
question of sovereignty, national pride, the flag. At its simplest Britain's claim is based on its citizens having occupied
the islands continuously, peacefully and effectively since
1833. In starkest terms the Argentines say the islands were
taken illegally and by force from the start, and they point to
their history books for "proof". There are plenty of "historical facts" to confuse the dispute. For nearly each and
every British claim, the Argentines will produce another one
of their own.

An Englishman called John Davis, an Elizabethan naviga-
tor and captain of the *Desire*, is credited with sighting the
islands in 1592 having been driven near them by a "sore
storm". Argentine history says there is no certainty as to the
date of discovery or the identity of the explorer but it
mentions Ferdinand Magellan and Amerigo Vespucci as
strong contenders. Among outsiders in the discovery stakes
are Vikings, Fijians or Chinese.

Certainly in 1690, nearly a hundred years after Davis
sighted the islands, another Englishman, John Strong, went
ashore from the *Welfare* to inspect penguins and thus made
the first known landing. Helpfully, he kept a record. He
sailed through the strait between the two main islands and
named it Falkland Sound after the third Viscount Falkland
who was a Commissioner of the Admiralty. Strong commented delightfully on the friendly reception accorded to his
men by the inhabitants, the penguins. "Upon some of our
men landing," he wrote, "they stood, viewed, and then
seemed to salute them with a great many graceful bows,
equally expressing their curiosity and good breeding."

The French were thereabouts too and the first to settle
among the penguins were intrepid Breton sailors from St

Malo who fished and hunted seals in those waters in the early eighteenth century. Thus a Paris map of 1722 called the islands *Isles Malouines* which in due course became the Spanish *Malvinas*, and ultimately the name the Argentines insist upon.

In 1764 the French established the first official settlement to serve as a staging post for their penetration of the Pacific. A fort was built and named Port Louis, some twenty miles north-west of today's capital. The Spanish, who claimed domination over all South America, except for those parts occupied by the Portuguese, were greatly displeased and so the French, preferring peace and some profit, sold the settlement to Spain for £25,000. Although the Argentines prefer not to remember it, Spain became the last of the three Great Powers of the seventeenth and eighteenth centuries to land on the Falklands. A Spanish Governor took over and gave Port Louis a new name, Puerto de la Soledad.

However the British had meanwhile been active in West Falkland with a landing by Commodore John "Badweather Jack" Byron, grandfather of the poet. His log records finding sorrel, celery, pelting some geese with stones and, more importantly, the establishment of a small settlement at Port Egmont. The visit led to a four-year row with the Spanish and eventually prompted the Spanish Governor in Buenos Aires to send a force of 1,400 to expel the British settlers. Outnumbered, the British surrendered, but the insult to the Union Jack brought Britain, France and Spain to the point of war. Spain tried to appease Britain by claiming that the Governor had been acting on his own initiative and without official instructions but a bitter diplomatic war of words ensued which aroused such passions in London that the government called on the leading polemicist of the day, Dr Samuel Johnson, to denigrate the Falklands. He produced a pamphlet entitled "*The thoughts on the late Transactions respecting Falkland's Islands*", in which he said it was clearly not worth fighting for "the empty sound of an ancient title to a Magellanic rock, an island thrown aside from human use, stormy in winter, barren in summer, an island which not even the

southern savages have dignified with habitation, where a
garrison must be kept in a state that contemplates with envy
the exiles of Siberia, of which the expense will be perpetual
and the use only occasional, a nest of smugglers in peace, in
war a refuge of future buccaneers."

In any event it was the French who made it clear they were
not prepared to go to war over the islands and three years
later, in 1771, Spain formally handed over Fort Egmont to
Captain Scott of the frigate *Juno*. This decision alone is seen
as a damaging blow to the Argentine claim of historical right
to the islands.

But within three years, the government in London, greatly
preoccupied with the rebellion in the North American col-
onies, swung round to the view that the cost of keeping a
settlement in the Falklands was disproportionate to its
value.

Lieutenant Samuel Wittewronge Clayton, the Governor of
Port Egmont settlement, was ordered to evacuate the islands
with his garrison. His last act was to affix a plaque to the door
of the clockhouse and hoist the Union Jack. The plaque read:

"Be it known to all nations that Falkland Islands with this
fort, the storehouses, wharves, harbours, bays and creeks
thereunto belonging are the sole right and property of His
Most Sacred Majesty George III, King of Great Britain,
Defender of the Faith, in virtue whereof this plate is set up
and His Britannic Majesty's colours left flying as a mark of
possession . . ."

The Spanish stayed on in East Falkland, using Puerto de la
Soledad as a prison settlement and ruling in somnolent
serenity. Buenos Aires appointed Governors until the
Napoleonic invasion of Spain. But by 1811, with Argentina's
fight for independence, Spain took no further interest. For

the next few years the islands were under no visible authority
and were used only by sealers, whalers and a few lawless
gauchos. Spain never reasserted her rights. That these rights
passed to Argentina automatically is a matter of assertion by
Buenos Aires as there was no direct transfer by the government in Madrid. According to Argentine history books,
Argentine "forces" occupied the Falklands in 1820.

But the man who has done the most to assist Argentine
claims to the Falklands, or at least to East Falkland, was a
Hamburg merchant of French descent named Louis Vernet.
Vernet established a settlement which lasted from 1826 to
1831 and in 1829, despite formal British protests, he managed to obtain the title of military and political Governor.
Vernet made money out of selling provisions to ships putting
in to Puerto de la Soledad and was also given exclusive
fishing rights. Then he made a major blunder by seizing the
schooners of the new power, the United States, in a dispute
over the fishing. The Americans promptly sent the USS
Lexington to Puerto de la Soledad, arrested six Argentines,
spiked the guns and destroyed the armaments, and declared
the islands free from all government.

The Buenos Aires government did not give up, and
appointed an interim Governor, Juan Mestivier, in place of
Vernet. There was a mutiny shortly after Mestivier's arrival
and he was murdered. Britain seized its chance and dispatched the sloop *Clio* to the islands to reassert sovereignty.
She arrived on New Year's day, 1833.

There are two versions of subsequent events. According to
Argentine history books the British sailors "brutally" expelled the Argentine garrison of fifty men at Puerto de la
Soledad. The British version is that there was merely a flag
incident when the Union Jack was raised and the "Buenos
Ayrean" flag was hauled down and handed over to the
Argentine commander. Certainly Britain had reasserted her
rights and without a shot being fired. In London the government claimed it was continuing the jurisdiction exercised in
the eighteenth century, that the rights of the Buenos Aires
government had never been recognised, and that there had

been protests made over the appointments of Vernet and
Mestivier.

The following year a British Governor was installed. It
was the start of continuous, unbroken British administration – until 2 April, 1982.

One other incident has found its way into Argentine
mythology, which purportedly proves the existence of guerrilla activity by patriotic Argentines against the British
invaders. When the Argentine garrison withdrew, its commander appointed a gaucho as Buenos Aires' representative.
But on 23 August, 1833, he and a British manager were
murdered by another gaucho named Antonio Rivero and
some convicts, who stole what they could and fled into the
interior. The party were hunted down by the Royal Marines
and Rivero had a spell in Newgate Prison before being
allowed to return to the River Plate. Today Rivero is considered as an Argentine hero, leader of a popular guerrilla
uprising. Squares have been dedicated to his memory, and a
statue was erected at Rio Gallegos, the nearest point in
Argentina to the Falklands. Plans were laid long ago to move
it to the capital of the *Islas Malvinas*.

Argentina allowed nearly fifty years to elapse after the
garrison's expulsion before reopening the question of sovereignty. Britain was informed that as Argentina was "con-
solidating and rounding off its territory", the Falklands
should be handed back by reason of the geographical position. London took little or no notice apart from pointing out
that under English occupation the Falklands had become a
"peaceable and prosperous settlement". For by then the
settlers had arrived along with their Cheviot sheep. The
Falkland Islands Company had steadily bought up sheep-
grazing land, built houses and stores. There was a thriving
trade in repairing and victualling with fresh meat and water
the great sailing ships heading for Cape Horn.

The Falklands had their first experience of naval action
in December 1914, but the enemy was Germany and not
Argentina. The German East Asia Squadron, under the
command of Vice Admiral Graf Maximilian von Spee, had

been making its way across the Pacific, determined to run the British blockade. Von Spee had stopped to raid Tahiti and was eager to snap up targets of opportunity on the long voyage home.

On 1 November this squadron, consisting of the heavy cruisers *Scharnhorst* and *Gneisenau* and three light cruisers, crushed a weak British cruiser squadron, sinking the *Good Hope* and the *Monmouth* at the Battle of Coronel off the South Chilean coast. In two hours of fighting the Royal Navy lost 1,000 men and boys. But revenge was only a month away. Shocked by the defeat, Winston Churchill, First Lord of the Admiralty, dispatched within a week a task force based on two modern battle cruisers, as superior in speed and armaments to the German cruisers as they had been to the *Good Hope* and the *Monmouth*. One of them was the *Inflexible* and the other, by a coincidence of traditional naval naming, was the *Invincible*.

Joined by five cruisers and commanded by Vice Admiral Sir Frederick Sturdee, they steamed at full speed for the Falklands where they were coaling in harbour when von Spee's ships were spotted twenty miles away. No record exists of von Spee's intentions. One theory is that he thought they were unguarded and decided to seize them for German supporters in Argentina and Brazil. His surprise at finding the British ships in the Falklands was complete. If he had taken the opportunity to attack while Sturdee's ships were still in harbour he might have scored a famous victory, but he turned away. The British fleet then steamed out and annihilated the German squadron. Von Spee died with his two sons and some 2,500 German sailors. This time only six British sailors were killed.

A monument to the action was erected near Stanley. It thanks Vice Admiral Sturdee for saving the colony from invasion and carries the legend: "Peace, Victory, War and Constancy."

The Falklands had not lost their strategic importance when the Second World War broke out. It was one of the bases in the hunt for the commerce-raiding battleship, *Graf*

Spee, which had been named after the man who triumphed at
Coronel and died at the Battle of the Falklands. When the
Graf Spee ran to seek refuge in Montevideo before being
scuttled, HMS *Exeter*, which had been hit by over a hundred
of the *Graf Spee*'s shells, limped off to the Falklands with her
fifty-three dead and many wounded.

A garrison of two thousand infantrymen and anti-aircraft
gunners had been sent to the Falklands at the beginning
of the war to protect them from occupation by any South
American country which might have decided to throw in
its lot with Nazi Germany – and the German influence in
Argentina was very strong. It was essential that the islands
remained in British hands in order to protect the vital sea
route round Cape Horn.

It was not until after the war, when the British garrison
had sailed home that the Argentine demagogue, Juan
Domingo Peron, who was elected President in 1946, realised
that he could use the Falklands issue as a means of boosting
his popularity. Slogans and rhetoric were the weapons of his
nationalism and state socialism, and one of the slogans of the
day was "Englishman, give us back the Malvinas". He also
moved on the diplomatic front: whenever Argentina signed
diplomatic treaties, especially those with other South American states, it would insist on appending a reservation pointing out that it contested British sovereignty over the islands.

Peron was deposed and driven into exile in 1955, but his
successors continued to press for the "return" of the Falklands. And in 1965 the United Nations were persuaded
by Buenos Aires to invite Britain and Argentina to begin
talks which would lead to a peaceful solution of the issue.
They can be said to have started slowly with the only flurry of
excitement being a brief Argentine comic-opera "invasion"
when a group of twenty young nationalists mounted "Operation Condor". They hijacked an aircraft, landed it on the
islands and raised the Argentine flag. (It has since been
suggested that some of those involved joined the anti-
government guerrillas in the 1970s and were killed by extreme right-wing death squads.)

By this time the Foreign Office in London was beginning
to think seriously about the future of the Falklands and
between 1971–73 agreements were made with the Argentines: on communications, postal services, travel, medical
facilities, education and customs measures. In the spirit of
the new relationship the Argentines finally established a
beach-head. Some forty workmen and technicians arrived at
Stanley to construct an airstrip. The men sailed from the
mainland aboard the *Cabo San Gonzalo* and were bid god-
speed by the then British Ambassador, Sir Michael Hadow.
They took with them 900 tons of Argentine equipment, a fact
which prompted a Buenos Aires magazine to comment that
"each item in a certain way implies the ratification of
Argentina's sovereignty". True or not, it was certainly a
considerable advance from five years previously, when the
Buenos Aires Post Office refused to accept letters posted from
the Falklands.

In fact 1972 was not a bad year for Anglo-Argentine
relations as they affected the Falklands. Argentine liners
began calling at Stanley with tourists, eight young Falklanders won scholarships to study in Buenos Aires secondary
schools, Argentine airline officials opened an office and took
up residence.

In 1974 there were further agreements on sea transport
links and on fuel supplies, but at the same time a new
propaganda campaign calling for an invasion of the islands
was being whipped up in the Buenos Aires press. London
ignored it, as it had done on other occasions.

Two years later the Argentines took offence over Britain's
decision to send an economic mission to the Falklands
headed by Lord Shackleton, son of the explorer. The mission
was given the job of reporting on the islands' problems and
potential, and to the Argentines it was a "provocation". The
upshot was that the Argentines did everything they could to
block the mission. A destroyer, the *Almirante Stormi*, even
attacked the research vessel *Shackleton* because it mistakenly
thought the noble Lord was on board.

The Shackleton report ran to 400 pages and its ninety

recommendations ranged from a proposal to extend the airstrip near Port Stanley to details about the grasslands scheme. The majority of the proposals were implemented, but the government could not find the money to extend the runway for use by aircraft other than those used by the Argentine Air Force. It would have cost just over £5 million.

In 1977 the question of the transfer of sovereignty was formally discussed in the British–Argentine talks for the first time. Three years later, in New York, Mr Nicholas Ridley, then Foreign Office Minister of State, floated the idea of a "leaseback" option to end the fifteen-year-old dispute. The plan called for Britain to hand over sovereignty to Argentina which would immediately lease the islands back for Britain to administer. Ridley, and the Foreign Office whose proposal it was, genuinely believed that the leaseback deal would secure the islanders' way of life and British control and administration, and it would also spur economic development.

Ridley flew to Stanley from New York to explain his proposals and was given a rough reception by the islanders, although he insisted that they would have the last word. He was also savagely attacked in the Commons. The Argentines also opposed the proposals. Whether they saw them as a sign that Britain was coming round to the idea of ridding itself of the Falklands is open to speculation.

There were further talks in 1981, but the Argentines rejected a British proposal for a freeze on the dispute for an agreed period while the two countries cooperated on developing the islands' resources. In New York on 26 and 27 February this year (1982) there was another formal negotiating session on the future of the Falklands. Before the talks had begun there were heavy hints in the Argentine press that Britain would be given an ultimatum: either agree to a firm timetable for handing over the islands, or face some kind of military action to recover them. It can be assumed that the Foreign Office knew of this pre-negotiation pressure but dismissed it as yet another insubstantial threat.

In New York the tone of the Argentine delegation of senior

diplomats was most cordial and friendly. The British team, headed by Mr Richard Luce, Foreign Office Minister of State, and including two members of the Falkland Islands Council who had taken part in earlier negotiations, thought the talks had gone rather well.

There were no threats from the Argentines about an invasion. But they did press for quick results. They requested monthly meetings at ministerial level, with the question of sovereignty to dominate the agenda. The British side was unenthusiastic about such frequent meetings and did not want to be too rigid over what should be discussed. So the talks ended amicably enough with a bland communique stressing how cordial and useful they had been.

But when the Argentine delegation returned home a different line was put out. A statement protested that Argentina had negotiated for fifteen years with patience, fidelity and good faith – all to no avail. More and more diplomatic gossip circulated in Buenos Aires to the effect that the junta was considering a wide range of options for "unilateral action" because of Britain's failure to make concessions. Among the options were initiatives in the United Nations, a diplomatic break, and in the final analysis, an invasion.

It was precisely the sort of gossip British diplomats had been listening to for years. Surely it was the Argentines crying wolf yet again: more brinkmanship, Argentine style.

2

THE SCRAP MERCHANTS ARRIVE IN SOUTH GEORGIA

At nine a.m. on Friday, 18 March, the *Bahia Buen Suceso*, a drab 3,100 ton Argentine Navy transport ship, slipped into Leith, a harbour on South Georgia island in the South Atlantic, and tied up at the wharf. Wearing fur-lined anoraks against the cold wind, the crew numbering some 100 officers and men, and a group of forty-two Argentine scrap merchants, busied themselves unloading tools and food and supplies for a long stay.

Some of the men carried guns ostensibly to shoot rats and other vermin because Leith, once a thriving base for whaling men from all over the world, was abandoned in 1964. Now it was a ghost village and harbour. There were sunken steam-driven whale catchers, and rusting and corroding iron chains, winches and sheds. There were large copper vats, huts and buildings that had housed the whalers and sealers, a fully-equipped hospital and, according to some, a veritable Aladdin's cave of stores and supplies. But nobody lived in Leith any longer.

During that weekend the scrap merchants made themselves at home. Stripping Leith was going to be a long hard job and winter would soon be drawing in. Some of the party decided to stock up with venison and went off to shoot wild reindeer – descendants of animals introduced from Scotland in 1911. They should not have done it. The deer were being studied by members of the British Antarctic Survey at nearby Grytviken and to all intents and purposes they were protected species.

Other Argentines, possibly sailors from the Canadian-built *Bahia Buen Suceso*, ran up the white and blue Argentine flag. Perhaps they felt that Leith, which had driven men to drink and suicide, needed cheering up, a splash of colour. They should not have done that either. South Georgia, 100 miles long and twenty miles wide, some 800 miles south-east of the Falklands, was a British dependency named by Captain Cook when he first landed there in 1775.

The man behind the enterprise was Constantino Sergio Davidoff, who seemed to have the blessing of the Argentine government and the British Foreign Office. Davidoff, a well-known Buenos Aires businessman, decided as long ago as 1978 that rich pickings were to be had on South Georgia. He contacted the Edinburgh Shipping firm Christian Salvesen, which owned the South Georgia whaling stations and offered to remove the scrap. In September 1979 he concluded a four-year contract said to involve "tens of thousands rather than hundreds of thousands of pounds" to dismantle and carry away some 35,000 tons of scrap worth at that time some £8 million. In December last year he went to South Georgia to inspect the stations and began drawing plans for stripping Leith. Curiously, the contract was due to run out in March, so Davidoff, having left it until the last minute, managed to get an extension of one year.

The Foreign Office knew of the contract, and raised no objection. It was, on the surface, a straightforward commercial deal. But the British Embassy in Buenos Aires was not at all pleased when Davidoff told them he had gone to South Georgia to have a look round because he had not told them in advance. Davidoff was told that he should seek their permission prior to any proposed subsequent visits.

Britain's biggest diplomatic and military humiliation since Suez – the occupation by Argentina of the Falkland Islands and South Georgia – came about because Davidoff, wittingly or unwittingly, ignored what he had been told. The Argentine scrap merchants were illegal immigrants. That weekend Mr Steven Martin, twenty-nine, of the British Antarctic Survey, magistrate and British administrator of

South Georgia, trekked for two hours with a few colleagues across the rough terrain to Leith from the British Antarctic Survey base at Grytviken, five miles away, to find out what was going on. Cordially but firmly he turned down the offer of a drink and some venison stew, and told the Argentines they required permission to stay. He also told them to take down the flag.

Martin returned to his base and radioed Stanley about the incident. He was told the Foreign Office would deal with the problem, and was asked to keep an eye on the Argentines in the meantime. The *Bahia Buen Suceso*, having unloaded eighty tons of materials, sailed off on Monday, to continue her routine run around Argentine ports and bases in the South Atlantic. Ten salvage merchants stayed on and set to work gathering coils of chains. They could not have known that their presence was giving rise to concern 8,000 miles away in London as it dawned – albeit slowly – on the Foreign Office that it had a ticklish little diplomatic problem on its hands.

Mr Anthony Williams, British Ambassador in Buenos Aires, went round to the Argentine Foreign Ministry in the San Martin Palace, and complained. He presented his complaints but pointed out that there had been an illegal landing at Leith and some Argentines were still there without permission. Williams' approach was low-key but the point had been made.

In the Commons Mr Richard Luce, Foreign Office Minister of State, said Britain would defend the Falklands and its dependencies "to the best of our ability", and that arrangements were being made for the "early departure" of the scrap merchants.

The incident seemed to have caused little excitement in either London or Buenos Aires. True, two Conservative MPs, Sir John Biggs-Davison and Mr John Stokes, said the landing was "provocative" and that it carried the gravest implications. The *Daily Telegraph*, whose coverage both before and after the 2 April invasion was unrivalled, gave the story considerable play. But generally very few people were impressed or frightened by a bunch of Argentine scrap merchants.

However the Royal Navy's Antarctic patrol ship *Endurance* was told to sail from Stanley to South Georgia with its normal compliment of Royal Marines. Sending the *Endurance* caused considerable embarrassment to the government and particularly the Ministry of Defence, for the 3,600 ton vessel was making its last patrol in the South Atlantic before being withdrawn for scrap as an economy measure designed to save about £2 million. (Predictably the government's earlier announcement that she was to be axed had been greeted with glee by the Argentine press.)

However when the *Endurance* arrived off Leith harbour with its twenty-two Marines, two Wasp helicopters and two 20mm guns, no action was taken. The Foreign Office was pursuing "diplomatic initiatives" and in the meantime *Endurance* was instructed to sit off South Georgia.

Then another ship appeared on the horizon – *Endurance*'s Argentine twin, the Polar transport *Bahia Paraiso*, also red-hulled for easy identification in the ice. It also carried Marines and two helicopters, and was armed with light cannon. It slipped into Stromness Bay and offloaded oil drums, a generator and other equipment.

In Buenos Aires a much tougher tone was being adopted and Williams was told that the Argentine party on South Georgia would be given "full protection". He was now reduced to pleading with Argentine Foreign Ministry officials that the way to solve the problem was for the scrap merchants to visit Grytviken base and complete immigration procedures, or alternatively the magistrate would go to Leith. It was a waste of breath. Realising they were dealing with a Britain preoccupied with crime figures, the Hillhead by-election and the forthcoming European summit, while Lord Carrington was enmeshed in critical Middle East talks, the junta in Argentina saw its chance.

Had they not been patient for too long with Britain over the *Malvinas*? Had they not said clearly and unequivocally on several times since the talks in New York in February that

there must be a firm timetable for handing over the *Malvinas*?
Had not Senor Alejandro Orfila, the Argentine General
Secretary of the Organisation of American States, declared
that the "Argentine flag would soon fly over the *Malvinas*"?
Had the British not failed to notice the Argentine Air Force
Hercules which landed in the second week of March at the
airport near Stanley, to test the feasibility of landing troops
on the island? Last but not least, Argentina was in economic
trouble which demanded drastic measures. A popular foreign policy adventure would distract the masses, if only for a
while.

Contingency plans for an invasion of the Falklands had
been drawn up by President Leopoldo Galtieri, Admiral
Jorge Anaya, the Navy chief, and General Basilio Lami
Dozo, who was the junior member of the triumvirate and
who represented the Air Force. Now, hearing from Foreign
Minister Nicanor Costa Mendez about the problem with
Britain over the scrap merchants, President Galtieri decided
to act.

On or about Friday, 26 March, the representative of
Britain's Secret Intelligence Service in Buenos Aires heard
about intense activity at Argentine naval bases. He may even
have been told by a source inside the Argentine power
structure that the plan to invade the Falklands was about to
move from hypothesis to implementation.

His report was sent in code from the British Embassy with
a degree of urgency. When it was read, and how soon it was
acted upon may never be known. But the Argentine fleet
movements were an open secret. British newspapers on
Sunday and Monday reported that the two 950 ton missile-
carrying Argentine corvettes, *Drummond* and *Granville*, were
on their way to "protect" the *Bahia Paraiso* anchored off
Leith. Three other ships were on the move that weekend
including the aircraft carrier *Veinticinco de Mayo* and two
escort vessels. They were carrying marine commandos and
paratroopers, and few seriously believed the claim that they
were on their way to take part in an exercise with the
Uruguayan Navy.

Such was the ignorance about Argentine intentions in
Whitehall that weekend that the Foreign Office announced
the reports were "blown out of all proportion". The Defence
Ministry reported that it had no knowledge that the Argentine Navy had cancelled all leave and said: "That is a matter
for the Argentines." This gave the impression that Mr John
Nott, the Defence Secretary, had heard nothing from his two
senior defence attachés in Buenos Aires.

The Ministry did acknowledge one item of news which had
come from Montevideo during the weekend: that forty-one
Royal Marines were on their way to the Falklands in the
Antarctic survey ship *John Biscoe* after being flown to the
Uruguayan capital. There was nothing "sinister" about it,
the spokesman hurried to say. It was "sheer coincidence"
that the Marine detachment already on the Falklands was
coming to the end of its twelve-month stint and was to be
relieved at the beginning of April. Therefore he could deny
that Britain was doubling its military strength in the Falklands.

It can be said that Whitehall did its best not to raise
tensions or give the Argentines any reason to complain of
provocative British actions. In fact the following day – when
it was brought home to the government that something
serious was happening – the Foreign Office said there was
nothing new to report and that diplomatic negotiations were
continuing.

What President Galtieri was making of the British reaction
as he boldly perfected plans for the invasion can only be
guessed. He may have thought it was a cunning British trick
to lure him into a false sense of security. But in London
President Galtieri's message was actually getting across. Mrs
Thatcher and Lord Carrington, Foreign Secretary, flew to
Brussels together for a crucial meeting of the European
Economic Community leaders which was to be dominated
once again by the problem of Britain's contribution to the
Community budget. Intelligence reports about the Falklands were read in the aircraft and as Lord Carrington said
later, "We had got firm information something might hap-

pen." He decided that it was time to make an urgent
statement in the House of Lords. Instead of going to Israel for
a two-day visit directly from Brussels, he flew to London to
tell the Lords that a "potentially dangerous" situation had
arisen. The unauthorised presence of the scrap merchants on
South Georgia was "not acceptable" and a further escalation
of the dispute was in nobody's interest. Britain would pursue
a diplomatic solution to the problem. From London he flew
off to Israel.

Britain also took its first small but most positive step: a
reprieve was announced for the *Endurance* which was still
shadowing the *Bahia Paraiso* off South Georgia, having seen it
land jeeps and men at Leith. There was also a report that the
nuclear-powered submarine *Superb*, 4,500 tons, was on its
way to the Falklands. It was a classic piece of disinformation.
The *Superb* was later seen at its base in Scotland, and it was
unlikely that any British submarine was in the South Atlantic at that time.

As the storm clouds gathered the Foreign Secretary was
discussing the Middle East and Palestinian autonomy in
Jerusalem with Mr Begin, the Israeli Prime Minister. It was
an important visit because Anglo–Israeli relations had been
going through a sticky patch, and clearly it was thought that
Britain's dispute with Argentina was not so serious as to
demand Lord Carrington's presence in London. However,
strong criticism was mounting from both sides of the House
of Commons as to why the government had been taken off its
guard in the South Atlantic.

Meanwhile, some 9,000 miles away, in the Globe, one of
the three Stanley pubs, islanders and Marines were jostling
for position at the bar. One of the regulars, sixty-five-year-
old Dave Stewart, summed it up for anyone prepared to
listen. "We want help," he said. "Remember we are British
to the backbone and we intend to stay that way. Don't let the
Argies take us over."

The very next day, April Fools Day, the Falklanders and
the British government both learned that the momentum
of events had escalated rapidly. The Cabinet Information

Committee told the Prime Minister that Argentine naval movements had put the fleet in a position to invade, and that invasion was inevitable.

Mrs Thatcher called a crisis meeting at her room in the Commons lasting from seven p.m. to midnight. The notable absentee was the Foreign Secretary, Lord Carrington, who was flying back from Israel in his VC 10.

By then it was too late for immediate and effective military action. *Endurance* had disembarked its detachment of twenty-two Royal Marines at Grytviken on the South Georgia coast and was on its way back to the Falklands. Even at a constant 13 knots it would take about two and a half days to reach Stanley.

There were no military options available. Royal Navy ships exercising off Gibraltar were still more than a week's sailing away. In any case they lacked air cover and were not capable of launching an amphibious landing. The main body of the fleet – including key ships such as the aircraft carriers *Invincible* and *Hermes* – were still in British waters. Nor could the Air Force help. The Hercules C130 transport aircraft could fly paratroopers down to Ascension Island but Stanley's airstrip was in Argentine hands. They would be useless. All that was left for the British government was to launch a diplomatic offensive. Mrs Thatcher telephoned President Reagan and urged him to intervene with Galtieri. The American President was alerted to the danger by his own intelligence reports from Buenos Aires as well as by the urgent diplomatic messages from London. At 20.20 hours Washington time on 1 April, while the Argentines were launching their operation, he made a personal telephone call to President Galtieri to express his deep concern and his hope that hostilities could be prevented.

It was a head of state to head of state call of dramatic length, even though half of the fifty minutes it lasted was taken up with English/Spanish translation. The Argentine leader's failure to take his strongly-worded advice clearly annoyed Mr Reagan, and he said of the invasion the following day, "I wish it had not gone forward." In Washington

there was nothing but annoyance that despite all efforts
America's principal ally in Europe and a leading pro-
Western country of Latin America were still on collision
course. The strongest words were reserved for Argentina
when the State Department issued a statement following
several discussions between Mr Alexander Haig, the Secretary of State, and Sir Anthony Parsons, Britain's representative at the UN. "We have told the government of Argentina
that we deplore the use of force to resolve the dispute. We call
on Argentina to immediately cease hostilities and to withdraw its forces from the Falkland Islands."

Later in New York, Sir Anthony Parsons called for an
emergency session of the UN Security Council. He said the
British government was a serious government and "we don't
make a practice of imagining totally groundless threats. We
don't make a practice of calling emergency meetings of the
Security Council." But Britain believed an armed attack on
the Falklands was imminent, and he asked what the United
Nations was going to do about it.

As President Galtieri met with his chiefs of staff and
worked out the final details of the invasion, the Governor of
the Falklands, Mr Rex Hunt, made a late-night broadcast to
the Falklanders. He said he might be forced to declare a state
of emergency before dawn. The island's garrison of eighty
Royal Marines was put on full alert. Members of the 120-
strong Falkland Islands Defence Force were called up. The
islanders were told to keep off the streets, stay away from
Stanley airport and not to stage demonstrations.

In the age of the nuclear superpowers the stage was set for
an old-fashioned territorial war between the one-time mis-
tress of the seas and a faraway country.

The fight for the Falklands was about to start in earnest.

3

THE JUNTA

Lieutenant General Leopoldo Fortunato Galtieri made his military reputation in the brutal and bloody anti-terrorist and guerrilla campaigns which amounted to a civil war in Argentina in the 1970s. It was his successes against the home-grown Marxist–Leninist enemies of his country which made it possible for him to become President and leader of the military ruling junta.

Until that point his life story had been the conventional one of a son of a modest family of Italian immigrants seeking fame and fortune in the army. He was born in Caseros on 15 July, 1926. Because he showed some technical aptitudes as a young man he was chosen for the Argentine Military College where he specialised in engineering, as a result of which in 1960 he was sent on an advanced course at Fort Belvoir in Virginia, USA.

Leopoldo Galtieri took to the Americans and they liked him for his rugged appearance – he might almost be mistaken for a Texan – his hard drinking and manly ways. During his North American stay he adopted as his military hero General George Patton, the famous "blood and guts" Army commander of the Second World War. In his fantasy life he saw himself clearly in such a role (though it was not an easy one to fulfil in the Argentine Army which had not been engaged in any war in the twentieth century) and his friends believe that it was for this reason that he transferred from the engineers to the cavalry, clearly a more dashing arm in its armoured form. They also say that he still seems more natural on a horse than behind a desk.

The top brass in the Argentine Army are traditionally

those of Italian descent and Galtieri ascended the ranks of the professional Army fairly painlessly. But his chance to display military talents did not arrive until the 1970s, by which time he was a field officer. The Peron era was finally coming to an end with the deposition of his widow, and while senior officers plotted to seize political power in Buenos Aires, guerrilla and terrorist groups were bringing chaos in the cities and out in the provinces. They were often all lumped together as the *Montoneros*. In fact the true *Montoneros* were leftist supporters of the old Peron regime who had dedicated themselves to a war of liberation to bring about a socialist revolution. Sometimes they worked alone and sometimes in conjunction with a like-minded group known as ERP (the Revolutionary People's Front) which mounted a powerful campaign of urban terror and guerrilla warfare in the countryside.

As their ruthless campaigns of murder and kidnap in the towns and their "Che Guevara"-style open assaults in the country brought fear and confusion in Argentina, the Army was called in to take counter insurgency action. Galtieri was posted to the north-western province of Tucuman which borders Chile. In the mountains and jungles of that region strong groups of the ERP tried to establish what they called a liberated area. It was from the headquarters at San Miguel that Galtieri commanded the troops which defeated guerrilla forces operating up to battalion strength, killing an estimated 600.

Those actions were the making of General Galtieri. He subsequently carried out police operations and broke the terrorist movements by brutal methods. His officers seized and tortured suspects and imprisoned hundreds, and it is said that Galtieri personally supervised many interrogations.

After General Roberto Videla seized power by coup d'état in 1976, Galtieri moved to the centre for Army operations which at the time were largely concerned with anti-terrorist actions. He was one of the Army corps commanders chosen by the military regime to take charge of five important towns. As commander of the Second Corps he was placed in control of Rosario, not far from the capital, which became a notorious centre of repression. The Second Corps has since been blamed for its use of torture and for the so-called "disappearances". Thousands of young men and women believed by the authorities to have been connected with the terrorists have literally disappeared. Estimates of their numbers vary between 6,000 and 15,000 and even as Argentinians were on the streets celebrating the capture of the Falklands, mothers of the "disappeared ones" were still parading silently behind their placards asking for news of their sons and daughters.

After four years of campaigning in what developed into a civil war, Leopoldo Galtieri was promoted in 1980 to Commander in Chief. Among fellow officers he was a popular figure, although some criticised his heavy drinking and he was known in senior officers' messes as "*Etiqueta*", after a popular brand of whisky drunk by the military. A bluff fellow given to impulsive judgments and to simplifying complicated arguments, he looked well in his American-style uniform and it was in barrack discussions of questions of the day that his first political ambitions were formed.

Critics unkindly gossip that when senior officers were discussing whether or not General Viola should succeed General Videla as President, Galtieri was so "fatigued" and incoherent that the meeting had to be postponed. Nevertheless he cultivated the friendship of senior officers including that of his old school classmate Admiral Jorge Anaya, Commander in Chief of the Navy, who is the descendant of a Basque family, and a member of the present junta. When he became Commander in Chief of the Army, Galtieri set about building himself up as a popular figure. He also began to establish himself as an officer known and trusted by the military in the US, making two visits there last year. The big, burly six footer with blue eyes, a mane of white hair, a soldier's soldier with a boxer's nose, speaking the language of the barracks, drinking and joking, he was an acceptable figure among military men.

On an official ten-day visit to the United States in the summer of 1981 he made the right noises in Washington

about Argentina and the US having "a joint mandate" to
work against the Marxist offensive in Latin America. He
reminded the administration that it was his Army which had
provided intelligence units and other help to El Salvador,
Guatemala and Honduras. Galtieri was paving the way to
becoming President and believed that he would have the
backing of Washington.

A few months later, on 22 December, 1981, having carefully prepared the ground in consultation with his military
cronies, General Galtieri pushed aside the ailing General
Viola and became President of Argentina. He announced
that he intended to work for a greater Argentina, saying:
"We do not want just a country, but a great country; we do
not want just a nation, but a great nation." In his mind he
was already thinking of means to increase the power and
prestige of his country by restoring to it the *Islas Malvinas*
which, as a hard-nosed patriot, he was convinced that the
British had wrongly taken away from Argentina.

During his talks with the Americans there had been
mention of the possibility of creating a South Atlantic
Alliance with the participation of South Africa to prevent the
Soviet Union spreading its influence in that strategic area.
The Americans were thinking in terms of preventing Russia
from increasing its grip on the Antarctic and halting the
spread of left-wing activity in Latin America. But Galtieri
might have formed the impression that they would, in return
for his friendship and alliance, give their support to seizure of
the Falklands.

In Buenos Aires, as the crowds cheered in the new President, few paid heed to the words of an opposition leader,
Francesco Manriques of the Federal Party, who declared,
"You are not seeing a transfer of power, but a transfer of
anarchy."

Cultivating the image of the simple soldier come to power
to rescue a nation from apathy, the new President publicly
declared his personal assets, and valued them at 180,000
dollars. Sceptical Argentines are well aware that the military
are heavily involved in high finance and that many have

made their fortunes from wheeler-dealing on the military budget. He went on living in the Commander in Chief's house at the Campo de Mayo barracks, a more than comfortable residence, and commuted from there to Government House by helicopter. To make up for that he put on his civilian clothes, a rarish thing for the military caste in a country fond of uniforms, and walked about chatting up the populace. He offered barbecues to the citizens and in general worked hard at public relations.

But the economy was in tatters despite the sale last year of £1,420 million worth of meat and grain to the Soviet Union which did not conflict in the President's mind with the crusade against Communism. Circuses were needed to distract the population from the knowledge that inflation was running at over 130 per cent and that a million and a half of the work force in a population of only 23 million were idle. And the chosen circus was a military one in a small cluster of South Atlantic islands.

When he took office President Galtieri handed over control of the economy to Roberto Alemann, a liberal economist, who became Secretary of the Economy with wide powers. But the remedies he proposed were painful in the extreme, involving a freeze on the wages of civil servants and cuts in the bloated defence expenditure. Roberto Alemann kept his view fixed upon a foreign debt of 34 billion dollars, a huge budget deficit, and the fact that in one day the peso lost thirteen per cent of its value against the dollar.

The President was keeping his eyes upon the forty-five generals on whom his continuance in power finally depended, and his ears upon noises from the streets of Buenos Aires where Peronists in the still-powerful trade unions were making their opposition heard. On 30 March one of the most violent street demonstrations since Argentina became a military tyranny six years ago, took place in the capital. Despite the fact that the demonstration, called by the General Confederation of Labour, had been officially postponed to maintain a show of national solidarity, people still turned out. Although a proportion of the demonstrators screaming abuse at "military assassins" were there for political reasons, the majority were there to protest at economic hardships. The police went into action and hundreds of arrests were made. The junta was alarmed and divided.

By this time plans were in an advanced state of preparation for the assault on the Falklands. The junta was convinced that by raising the patriotic issue of possession of those islands it could distract the attention of the discontented population at home by offering them a great cause. In any case Costa Mendez, the Foreign Minister, felt sure that the British needed only an excuse to rid themselves of the Falklands.

There is now evidence that it was not President Galtieri, but his old schoolfriend and fellow member of the three-man junta, Admiral Jorge Isaac Anaya, who had made the running in stirring the Falklands affair. It was the Admiral who encouraged the Davidoff scrap metal expedition and who saw the possibility of exploiting the belated British reaction to it.

The Council on Hemispheric Affairs meeting held later in Washington claimed that in his capacity as Commander of the Argentine Navy, it was Admiral Anaya who took the initiative without prior consultation, ordering units of the fleet to sea. Led by the sole Argentine aircraft carrier, the *Veinticinco de Mayo*, a number of warships sailed from Puerto Belgrano. It was the view of the Council, a responsible body specialising in Latin American affairs which is sponsored by American trade unions and academic groups, that the Admiral dragged the Army and Air Force behind him. It further claimed that General Basilio Lami Dozo, commander of the Air Force, hesitated to commit his aircraft to the forthcoming battle.

It was not the first occasion upon which Admiral Anaya had pushed his fellow officers of the junta into action. In 1979 he was the man largely responsible for rekindling the old border dispute with neighbouring Chile over the ownership of the Beagle Channel. His privateering in the councils of state confirm the view that the junta is far from united on

policy-making decisions and that the senior officers of the
armed forces constantly curb and over-ride decisions by the
President. Under the military constitution, the President is
the servant of the heads of the three services.

It so happens that since General Galtieri became President, and unlike his predecessor, he has also been able to
retain his position as Commander in Chief of the Army,
pending his retirement next year. But the power of the
President is limited by the fact that a majority in the three-
man junta (an emotive word which seems redolent of Fascism
in English, but which in Spanish simply means committee),
can vote him out of office.

Apart from the junta, the President has his own cabinet of
eight ministers, most of them civilians such as the Foreign
Minister, Costa Mendez. Had the constitution been less
complex in its functioning, and had President Galtieri been
a true dictator, Mrs Thatcher's government might have
found it easier to negotiate with him. But the reality of the
situation was that Galtieri and his fellow officers did not
always think with one mind or even speak with one voice.

In the normal course of events President Galtieri and the
present junta will continue in office until March 1984. It is
one of those fatal dates beloved by Latin politicians, for the
year marks the 150th anniversary of the British establishing
themselves in the Falkland Islands.

To the generals and admirals who rule Argentina it all
looked very simple when their troops moved across the 400
miles of ocean separating their country from the Falklands.
They knew how little value the British placed upon the
islands and expected only a modest amount of protest and
finger-wagging from London.

4

THE ARGENTINE INVASION OF THE FALKLAND ISLANDS

At armed forces headquarters in Buenos Aires there was bustle and excitement as the time approached for the first landings of the Argentine task force on their *Malvinas*. But in the provincial atmosphere of Government House, Ross Road, Stanley, calm prevailed until four thirty p.m. on Thursday, 1 April. It was the calm of ignorance. At that time Governor Rex Hunt summoned to his office Dick Barker, chief secretary to the administration, Ronald Lamb, chief of police, and members of the executive council.

He had only just received a signal from the Foreign Office, belatedly warning him that an Argentine invasion force was heading for the Falklands. The estimate was that by dawn the following morning, Argentine warships would be off Cape Pembroke. Until that moment the only indication of approaching danger given to the authorities in the Falklands was that the Argentines were expected to put a landing party ashore from a submarine. They expected the operation to be similar to the one conducted by the scrap men in South Georgia.

To meet that minor threat Mr Hunt had consulted with the Major commanding the small detachment of Royal Marines at Stanley. They prepared a simple plan to deal with this small emergency. Corporal Carr with two Marines was to keep watch in the Cape Pembroke lighthouse and another lone corporal went as look-out to Sapper Hill. If they spotted a party coming ashore from a submarine, a reaction squad of Marines would be alerted to rush to the beach and arrest them.

In the light of the new and late information such a plan would have been absurd. Both the Governor and his military detachment had been badly informed and were at a disadvantage. Major Mike Norman had arrived to take command only two days earlier, and was in charge of the forty strong Marines group which had been flown into Montevideo, wearing civilian clothes and without weapons, for sea transport to Stanley, where they would relieve an outgoing force under Major Gary Noot. Because of the tension both groups had been ordered to stay on for the time being, though a Foreign Office briefer in London had told Major Norman that the Argentines were not going to invade.

It was good to have reinforcements by chance, but the old detachment was already below strength. As a result the only military force at the disposal of the Governor consisted of two Majors and some sixty fighting soldiers.

Mr Hunt, who is no stranger to barracks language, told them, "It looks as though the silly buggers mean it." The officers, with only sixteen hours to go before a large-scale invasion, set about organising their modest military resources for resistance. They had no time either to improvise booby traps for the airport runway, or to block the harbour entrance. They were short of material such as mines for the beaches. There were not enough small arms, and their only mortar was unserviceable. However, assuming that the Argentines would land from the sea, they selected the most likely beach in York Bay and there used up their total stock of barbed wire. Having done this, the whole force assembled in the evening to receive orders at their barracks at Moody Brook. Major Norman divided them into six sections, each under an NCO, and told them to keep hitting and running before a final withdrawal to Government House where a last stand was planned.

While they started their preparations Governor Hunt arranged to make a broadcast over the local radio to the 1,800 Falkland Islanders, with "an important announcement about the state of affairs between the British and Argentine governments over the Falkland Islands dispute."

The Governor's broadcast, greeted with incredulity in the islands, caused a sensation as the population listened, either in their agreeable, terraced wooden houses, or in the bar of such establishments as the Globe Inn. He told them, "There is mounting evidence that the Argentine armed forces are preparing to invade the Falklands." Unless the United Nations Security Council could arrange something quickly, a state of emergency might have to be declared. Meanwhile people should keep calm and stay off the streets. Even though the people of the Falklands had for years considered it possible that one day the "Argies" they so mistrusted might try to seize the islands by force, they could hardly believe that the day was about to dawn.

The Governor told Patrick Watts, who runs the radio station, to stay on the air until further notice, and promised the listeners that he would broadcast again as soon as there was anything to report. Meanwhile the hospital was being made ready by Stanley's three doctors with the help of a retired lady doctor.

Although he had not said so on the radio, the anxious Governor knew for certain that nothing could prevent a large-scale Argentine landing. Apart from the Marines, the only defence available was in the form of the Falkland Islands Defence Force, theoretically 120 strong, and its members were ordered to report to the Drill Hall. "We will have a crack at anything coming through the Narrows," added Mr Hunt, referring to the neck of water leading from Port William into Stanley Harbour. In such a homely place, where the population had good English names like Miller, Stewart, Biggs and Butler, these small preparations for war brought with them an air of unreality.

Mr Hunt appreciated the implications of the presence of seventeen Argentine gas workers in Stanley. Perhaps they were the Falkland version of the scrap men in South Georgia, secretly armed and only waiting for the right moment to hijack the Governor. Yet if he were to take any action against them, the Argentine government might well use the gas workers as a pretext to justify invasion.

So, quietly, and in the early hours of the morning, he had the unfortunate men rounded up and taken off to the Town Hall, where they were kept under lock and key. There were also deep suspicions about Vice Commodore Hector Gilobert of the Argentine Air Force, who had lived in Stanley for two years as the representative of LADE, the Argentine airline which ran a weekly flight service to the mainland. He was generally considered to be the unofficial representative of Argentina on the islands, and he had returned from a home visit the week before. Further inauspicious news came from an Argentine photographer on the Falklands. He reported that he had picked up a Buenos Aires broadcast announcing in Spanish: "From tomorrow morning, the *Malvinas* will be Argentine."

After midnight, the Governor was on the air again to say that the approaching ships had not changed course. The entire population was still listening when Mr Hunt reached for the microphone again at four twenty-five a.m. to announce that as the Argentine government had not responded to the Security Council order to refrain from invading, "I therefore have no alternative but to declare a state of emergency under the Emergency Powers Ordnance, 1939." He went on to explain that under the terms of the Ordnance he was now in charge as Commander in Chief, with power to issue any orders he thought fit.

By two a.m. the Marines were in position. The twenty or so members of the local home guard who had managed to reach the Drill Hall were put on duty at such places as the radio station. A small group of journalists, including Kenneth Clarke, correspondent of *The Daily Telegraph*, and Simon Winchester from *The Times* was positioned in an unoccupied house only a hundred yards from Government House. They were joined by Mr Don Bonner, steward to the Governor and driver of his official car. (Simon Winchester was later arrested in Argentina together with Ian Mather of the *Observer* and Tony Prime, a photographer. They were held in prison on charges of espionage.)

When the attack came its form surprised everybody. The

first 150 Argentine troops from their Marine special forces
landed not from the sea but by helicopter at Mullett Creek,
within striking distance of the Royal Marines, former HQ at
Moody Brook. Explosions rang out, followed by the sound of
automatic weapon fire, coming from very near Government
House.

Mr Hunt broadcast again at six a.m. announcing that
sixteen amphibious APCs were entering the Narrows. At
about the same time a seventy-strong group of Argentine
special forces, who had been landed by helicopter, carried
out a brisk SAS-style raid upon the Marines' barracks at
Moody Brook. Even though the place was empty they took
no chances and went in kicking down doors and hurling
grenades, following up their attack with bursts of automatic
weapon fire. Phosphorous grenades were also used.

There can be no doubt that the Argentines went in for the
kill, hoping to take the Royal Marines by surprise. Had the
Marines been in position there they would have sustained
heavy losses and the rest of the seaborne landing would have
taken place unopposed. From the Argentine point of view, it
was a well-conceived operation. Its planning may have owed
something to the fact that some Argentine special forces had
attended Special Air Service training courses in Britain. The
assault troops were all well equipped: their weapons were
fitted with flash eliminators, making it particularly hard for
the Marines to spot enemy fire positions.

A little while after the Moody Brook attack came the
assault on Government House. One team burst through the
rear perimeter wall, hurling stun grenades as they ran
towards the building. Royal Marine snipers caught them in
heavy fire and later they could see three Argentines in black
camouflage uniform lying motionless in the grounds. The
invading troops had also taken an old white building very
near Government House and the office of Cable and Wireless. Later Kenneth Clark recalled how, half-deafened by the
noise of the grenades, mortar bombs and firing, he heard
Argentine soldiers shouting to each other in Spanish before
crying out in English to the Governor: "Mr Hunt, surrender.

You are surrounded. The Marines are here. Can you hear us. You are a reasonable man. Surrender."

Each call was answered by bursts of small arms fire from the Royal Marines defenders, and at one point an English voice from the garden yelled back: "He does not surrender."

Patrick Watts was still manning the radio station and reporting developments as islanders telephoned in to tell him what was happening. "Armoured cars are coming up the hill," said one report. "There is plenty of firing," said another.

Remarkably, nobody was hurt in the crossfire even though houses along the road from the airport to Stanley were damaged by mortar fire and by cannon fire from personnel carriers. The radio repeated its warning that people should keep off the streets, particularly after one elderly man had been hauled back inside his home, protesting that he had to be out to start work early.

Mr Hunt, who had a link to the radio station, maintained his broadcasts and declared initially that he would not surrender to "the bloody Argies". However, telephone callers were reporting that the blue and white Argentine flag was flying over the airport; Patrick Watts suddenly went off the air, and his voice was replaced by an Argentine who formally addressed the "English colonial government of the *Malvinas*" and said that his side wished to avoid bloodshed. It became clear that the end was near.

At almost eight a.m. a man, bearing a white flag, was seen walking along Ross Road towards Government House. It was Vice Commodore Gilobert, who had come to act as mediator. At this stage, Major Norman recommended that the Marines in Government House, rather than staying in position until they were over-run, should break out and take the Governor with them. But Mr Hunt decided that the small force stood a poor chance of survival in face of such a powerful attacking force and that the time had come to give in. He made his way towards the Roman Catholic church in Ross Road where Argentine officers were waiting to accept his surrender. He refused to shake hands with General Oswaldo Jorge Garcia, who called himself the temporary military governor of the *Malvinas*. He also rejected a handshake from Admiral Carlos Busser, commander of the Argentine Marines, insisting that the invasion force had made illegal entry onto British territory. Mr Hunt called on his experience as a professional diplomat who had been present when the British Embassy had to be abandoned as the North Vietnamese surged into Saigon. All he could do was to maintain the dignity which the situation undoubtedly demanded.

The Royal Marine defenders were forced to hand over their weapons and lie face downward in the roadway outside Government House, before being herded under guard into the paddock nearby. Their injured pride was restored somewhat by the remarks of the Argentine Admiral Busser who described both the Governor and his troops as "courageous men" and explained, "We brought crushing superiority to prevent people getting hurt."

Casualties were indeed few and despite the large amount of ammunition expended, the British Marines claimed that they had killed only three of the attackers and had wounded three others. They also claimed that a landing craft had been destroyed with a shot from an anti-tank recoilless rifle. As the Falkland Islanders gradually emerged into the unusually bright sunshine on that Saturday morning, the new situation was clearly evident: they were living under a foreign occupying power. The young Argentine soldiers smiled and greeted them with hesitant attempts at "Good morning", but the build-up of military strength on the island had begun. Two thousand troops, well-equipped with amphibious armoured vehicles, were being brought ashore and a tank-landing ship steamed through the Narrows. A little later the Argentine Air Force staged a victory fly-past of a C130 escorted by four Pucara fighters.

Then Mr Hunt, grandly attired in his ceremonial diplomatic uniform, complete with plumed hat and sword, appeared outside, ready for the drive to the airport in his maroon taxi. A small Union Jack fluttered from the bonnet. His wife, Mavis, was in tears, but as they bade farewell to friends, the Governor promised, "We'll be back."

5

PANIC AND CONFUSION

Confused motives and failure to appreciate what might be the consequences of military action in the islands had driven the Argentine government to launch the invasion. In London the news was greeted with amazement. The public had no idea that such a crisis was about to burst and despite earlier warnings the Thatcher government seemed taken aback as it blundered into a shooting conflict. The first signs of bewilderment were apparent as ministers and officials, in a state of confusion and embarrassment, began to acknowledge what had happened.

Within an hour of the Argentine Marines landing at Stanley, seizing the airport and accepting Governor Hunt's surrender, the Argentine news agencies were putting out the first military communiques. The eighty-one Royal Marines were rounded up, Argentine warships sailed into the harbour and unloaded armoured and amphibious vehicles. Meanwhile in Buenos Aires the victory flags were raised and in London, an emergency Cabinet meeting was called at No 10 Downing Street. It was the first to be held on a Friday since the Rhodesian crisis in 1979. Present to brief ministers were the First Sea Lord, Admiral Sir Henry Leach, and the Chief of Air Staff, Air Marshal Sir Michael Beetham. The detailed account of Cabinet discussions will remain secret for at least thirty years and even then they may be edited if they involve especially sensitive security matters. (It is said that Sir Anthony Eden, the Conservative Prime Minister at the time of Suez, had key papers destroyed after the debacle.) But it can be assumed that the military chiefs told Mrs Thatcher, Lord Carrington and Mr John Nott, the Defence Secretary, of the disposition of the British Fleet, and made it clear that nothing could be done at that moment to reverse a stunning fait accompli.

In any case the government did not have access to clear information about what was going on in the Falklands. Nor was it disposed – quite rightly – to believe everything that was issued by the junta's propaganda machine. Such was the panic and confusion in Whitehall that its handling of the invasion news was a shambles, and unfortunately it did not improve as the crisis continued.

Mr Humphrey Atkins, Lord Privy Seal and Deputy Foreign Secretary, can be said to have begun the process when he went to the House of Commons – which meets in the morning on Fridays – to make a two-minute statement. He rose at eleven a.m. to declare in clipped and measured tones that the situation had become increasingly grave . . . there was now a very real expectation that an Argentine attack against the Falklands would take place very soon . . . Britain was taking appropriate military and diplomatic measures to sustain its rights under international law, and in accordance with the provisions of the United Nations charter . . . a further statement would be made to the House in the afternoon if necessary. With the Prime Minister sitting silently alongside him, he said he could not confirm reports that Argentine troops had landed on the Falklands, although half an hour previously the Governor had been in touch with the government but he had made no mention of an invasion.

The unfortunate Mr Atkins was forced to admit subsequently that he had made a mistake. No contact had been made between Whitehall and the Governor then. Rather, it had taken place at about eight thirty a.m. London time, just before the Argentine invasion, and all conventional communication links with the Falklands were cut some fifteen minutes later. As Friday wore on, Mr Atkins' mistake was compounded. At the Foreign Office's regular twelve thirty briefing for local and foreign journalists, a spokesman said there was no confirmation that any invasion of the Falklands had begun and he went on explicitly to deny a report on ITN's Oracle Service that the Foreign Office had said that it had. However, he did confirm that the Foreign Office was in touch with the British Ambassador in Buenos Aires who had issued "appropriate advice" to the 17,000 British subjects in Argentina. The FO spokesman also volunteered the information that it was "unlikely" that Lord Carrington would now be able to attend a special meeting of Common Market Foreign Ministers in Luxembourg.

It was a briefing given by an apparently calm, unruffled and confident diplomat. But this was the face of professionalism. In fact Whitehall was gripped by confusion, and a degree of panic. The FO would only confirm the invasion if officially informed that it actually happened by a reliable, on-the-spot source such as Governor Hunt or the Royal Marine commander on the Falklands, but now, of course, this was impossible. However somebody did telephone the Falkland Islands Office in London to see if there was an available list of radio hams on the islands. Inevitably, the question was asked: why had these inquiries not been made earlier, as a precautionary measure?

The news blackout continued well into the afternoon. Shortly before three p.m., Mr Francis Pym, then Leader of the Commons, made a short statement saying that the House would be recalled during the weekend "if the situation in the Falklands deteriorated", though he was still unable to confirm unofficial reports of the invasion.

Later, the Prime Minister consulted with Lord Carrington and Mr Nott, and a press conference was hastily called at the Foreign Office. Shortly after six p.m., looking very sombre and aware of the mounting political criticism of their policies, the two ministers officially admitted that the invasion had taken place, although still only few details about what had happened were available. They knew that Government House was surrounded by troops and armoured personnel carriers and that the Governor had been taken captive. They knew that the Argentine naval force comprised one light fleet aircraft carrier, one heavy cruiser, four destroyers (two of which were guided missile ships), three guided missile corvettes and three troop-carrying ships. Three Argentine submarines in the area were also believed to be on station.

At the press conference Mr Nott was asked whether the Marines had been given prior orders to surrender if faced with overwhelming odds. He replied that "the British never give orders to anyone to surrender" – an answer he had to amplify the following day to mean the Royal Marines never surrendered "without a fight". He announced that the Navy was assembling its own task force to sail to the Falklands, although it would take more than two weeks to arrive because of the 8,000 miles separating Britain and the Falklands. Also Britain had broken diplomatic relations with Argentina, giving her diplomats in London four days to leave.

Both ministers expressed surprise and distaste when asked if they were going to resign. Although they had been caught off guard, the invasion could have happened at any time in the last fifteen years and even if the task force had set sail for the area the day that the first scrap merchant had landed on South Georgia, it would not yet have arrived.

The two ministers were also asked whether Britain regarded the Argentine invasion as an act of war. Lord Carrington replied "Well, the answer to that is that under Article 51 of the United Nations Charter any state which is the victim of an armed attack has the inherent right of individual or collective self-defence until the Security Council has taken measures necessary to maintain international peace and security. And this right of self-defence clearly comprehends any military or naval action which might be necessary to repel or expel any invading force." For the first time, Britain had indicated officially its preparedness to fight to regain the Falklands.

A little later, a telex message from Stanley to London dramatically confirmed the government's worst fears that it had completely failed to assess which way a repressive and erratic right-wing military junta would jump.

London had spent hours trying to establish contact with the Falklands capital and suddenly it succeeded.

The London operator asked: "What are all these
    rumours?"
Stanley replied: "We have lots of new friends."
London: "What about these invasion rumours?"
Stanley: "Those are the friends I was meaning."
London: "They've landed?"
Stanley: "Absolutely!"
London: "Are you open for traffic?"
Stanley: "No orders on that yet. One must obey
                orders."
London: "Whose orders?"
Stanley: "The new Governor."
London: "Argentina?"
Stanley: "Yes."
London: "Are the Argentines in control?"
Stanley: "Yes. You can't argue with thousands of
                troops plus enormous Navy support when you
                are only 1,800 strong."

Just a few more words were sent over the teleprinter from
Stanley. They were routine. They signalled, "Stand by
please."
    Then the line went silent.

6

THE FIRST PARLIAMENTARY DEBATE: SATURDAY, 3 APRIL

The grave news from the Falklands created in Britain a mood of shocked disbelief and quiet anger of a kind and depth which the country had not felt at any time since the Second World War. It was so clearly an act of naked aggression. Argentine troops had landed upon and seized British territory, island territory moreover, and the British themselves were more comparable to those of the British in 1939 comparatively small island in a hostile world.

If the idea were allowed to get around that islands might be seized would not the British Isles themselves be in danger? That was the reasoning behind the mood of sober understanding. That is why the Falklands crisis was so different from any other of the dangerous affairs which had confronted the nation in recent years.

"Shamed!" screamed the headlines in popular newspapers. That was the melodramatic form. The true feeling was that an overwhelming majority wanted action to set things to rights in the Falklands. There was a consciousness that things had gone wrong, that warlike and unscrupulous people had taken advantage of unpreparedness and this could not be tolerated. George Gale put it well in the *Daily Express*, "If Argentina can shove us around, who cannot push us over?"

Never in recent foreign affairs crises had events taking place thousands of miles away produced such a spontaneous feeling of national solidarity in face of adversity. As people discussed aggression in the South Atlantic their reactions were more comparable to those of the British in 1939 when they quietly agreed that the Nazi Germans had gone far enough and must now be challenged with force. The scale of the thing was smaller but the feelings were familiar.

The mood was totally unlike that which prevailed at the time of the Suez crisis when the Conservative government of Sir Anthony Eden, who saw President Nasser as a re-incarnation of Hitler, ordered the armed forces to land at Port Said and seize the Suez Canal. At that time the country and the parties were riven into two noisy camps, one crying "War by Jingo", and the other, "Peace at any price". On this occasion few were in a mood to compromise and fewer still to side with President Galtieri. Even inveterate peace-mongers on the left were half inclined to agree that such obviously Fascist military rulers could not be allowed to have things their own way.

It was fascinating on that spring Saturday morning when the crisis blossomed to compare the public mood in Britain and in Argentina. In Buenos Aires the crowds could be observed marching, shouting and flag-waving in a delighted excess of jingoism. In London, under pale sunshine, there were no marchers. The biggest crowd in London gathered in a long and well-ordered queue for places in the public gallery of the House of Commons. These quiet people of all sorts wanted to be there for the occasion of the specially called Saturday debate and because they wanted to know what the government intended to do about the Falklands.

It was the first great parliamentary occasion in a major international crisis directly concerning Britain since the BBC had been authorised to place its microphones in the Chamber itself. It was possible therefore for the population at large to eavesdrop on the statements and on the debate within. The fact that ministers and Members of Parliament were aware that the nation was listening to them, and that they represented democracy at a difficult time, had a sobering effect upon the quality of the debate.

Mrs Margaret Thatcher began the exceptional proceedings quietly enough by reading in unemotional tones a carefully prepared brief. Only as she went along did she manage to convey a sterner tone and in her best headmistress

voice made the statement "Yesterday morning at 8.23 a.m.,
we sent a *telegram* . . ." sound decisive and foreboding. With
mounting confidence, even though she knew it would not be
long before the critics would be demanding resignations and
asking why things had gone so badly wrong, she assumed the
mantle of the "Iron Lady", a description of her coined by
Soviet propagandists. Loyal cheers began as she condemned
"this unprovoked aggression" which had "not a thread of
justification, nor a scrap of legality".

She said the Falkland Islands and the dependencies remained British territory, and that "no aggression and no
invasion can alter that simple fact. It is the government's
objective to see that the islands are freed from occupation
and are returned to British administration at the earliest
possible moment."

Mrs Thatcher continued by reviewing the history of the
dispute with Argentina over sovereignty, the fifteen years of
meetings, the bellicose Argentine press comment. The government had seen the landing of the scrap merchants on
South Georgia as a minor problem, but it had become clear
that Buenos Aires had little interest in trying to solve it.

The first jeers reverberated around the packed benches
when she tried to remind the House that the Argentines had
occupied Southern Thule (another South Atlantic dependency) in 1976 when the Labour government were in office,
and the House had not been told until two years later. Mr
Ted Rowlands, who was Labour's Foreign Office Minister
responsible for the Falklands at that time, was on his feet. He
said, "The right honourable Lady is talking about a piece of
rock in the most southerly part of the dependencies, which is
totally uninhabited and which smells of large accumulations
of penguin and other bird droppings. There is a vast difference – a whole world of difference – between the 1,800
people now imprisoned by Argentine invaders and that argument. The right honourable Lady should have the grace to
accept that."

Mrs Thatcher did not accept this but after Mr Rowlands'
intervention her speech continued at great speed. The point

was made that this debate in the House of Commons was not the place for scoring party political points. Even the most loyal of party hacks on both sides of the House were conscious of grave events and national consequences. They were in a mood to serve warning that ministers such as Lord Carrington, the Foreign Secretary, and Mr Nott, at the Defence Ministry, must go if it were proved that they had failed in their duty. In such a serious frame of mind members did not encourage party point scoring, as indeed Mr Nott discovered later in the debate.

For the moment Mrs Thatcher was content to outline her first plans for putting things to rights. The government had decided that a large task force would sail to the Falklands as soon as possible. Meanwhile it would continue diplomatic efforts, helped by its friends. Also Argentine banks' assets held in Britain would be frozen.

To cries of "resign" she finished: "The people of the Falkland Islands, like the people of the United Kingdom are an island race. They are few in number, but they have the right to live in peace, to choose their own way of life and to determine their own allegiance. Their way of life is British: their allegiance is to the Crown. It is the wish of the British people and the duty of Her Majesty's government to do everything that we can to uphold that right. That will be our hope and our endeavour and, I believe, the resolve of every Member of the House."

Now it was the turn of Mr Michael Foot, the Labour Opposition leader with a reputation for oratory, and he tore into the government, accusing it of betraying the Falklanders. He said the islanders looked to Britain for help at this moment of their desperate plight, just as they had looked to Britain for the last 150 years.

He said: "They are faced with an act of naked, unqualified aggression, carried out in the most shameful and disreputable circumstances. Any guarantee from this invading force is utterly worthless – as worthless as any of the guarantees that are given by this same Argentine junta to its own people.

"We can hardly forget that thousands of innocent people

fighting for their political rights in Argentina are in prison and have been tortured and debased. We cannot forget that fact when our friends and fellow citizens in the Falkland Islands are suffering as they are at this moment."

In his best speech since becoming leader of the Opposition, he concluded to loud cheers: "The government must now prove by deeds – they will never be able to do it by words – that they are not responsible for the betrayal and cannot be faced with that change . . ."

An equally fierce attack on the government came next from one of their own side, Mr Edward du Cann, Chairman of the Conservative 1922 Committee, who praised Mr Foot for his condemnation of Argentine aggression. He said it was "astounding" that Britain was so "woefully ill-prepared", "extraordinary" that conventional forces were not deployed on standby against an occupation, and "fatuous" to have thought the problem could be solved by only diplomatic means. He ended to a roar of "hear, hear": "Let us hear no more about logistics. About how difficult it is to travel long distances. I do not remember the Duke of Wellington whining about Torres Vedras. We have nothing to lose now except our honour."

Mr Enoch Powell, the Ulster Unionist MP and a former Tory minister, began by talking about Northern Ireland but emphasised: "There is only one reaction which is fit to meet unprovoked aggression upon one's own sovereign territory: that is direct and unqualified and immediate willingness – not merely willingness, but willingness expressed by action – to use force."

Mrs Thatcher had been called the Iron Lady, said Mr Powell. In the next week or two the nation would learn of what metal she was made. The Prime Minister looked at him, nodded slowly and appeared to say something in agreement.

A Conservative MP and former Foreign Office minister, Sir Nigel Fisher, provoked jeers and laughter when he said the very least Britain could do was to ensure the exclusion of Argentina from the World Cup.

Dr David Owen, a Social Democrat and a former Labour Foreign Secretary, called for the blockade of the Falklands backed up by the deployment of a hunter-killer submarine. He did not agree that it would have been absurd to have sent a force to the area a month ago.

It quickly emerged that the MPs had three targets in their sights: the Foreign Office, Mr Nott, and Argentina. There were also attacks on British Intelligence for "failing to detect" Argentine preparations for the invasion.

Mr Rowlands insisted that "our intelligence" in Argentina had always been extremely good, and he could not believe it had changed. He went on: "I shall make a disclosure. As well as trying to read the mind of the enemy, we have been reading its telegrams for many years. I am sure that many sources are available to the government, and I do not understand how they failed to anticipate some of the dangers that suddenly loomed on the horizon."

He claimed that in 1977 the Labour government had employed ships in the area because it had been led to believe there were going to be major problems in talks with Argentina about the Falklands. The Argentines backed away from a fight. The government's policy then was that it was better to be safe than sorry.

A Conservative MP, Mr Patrick Cormack, said Mr Foot had "truly spoken for Britain" and he added: "Someone has blundered. I do not know whom and I do not know how, but I have my suspicions, and they are directed inevitably – and regretfully – at both the Secretary of State for Defence and the Foreign Secretary."

Another Conservative backbencher, Mr Ray Whitney, who was a former diplomat, was roughly treated by his own side when he counselled understanding of the Argentine position and said Britain had to negotiate a peaceful settlement. Almost a lone voice, he called for careful consideration of the next moves. "The easy way would be to respond thoughtlessly," he said. "I should like to outline to the government the real problems that we will face when we move in.

"Are we ready as a nation, and shall we continue to be ready, to accept the military implications of what is involved in a landing on the islands? If we are, well and good, but are we ready to maintain that effort not for a week, not for a month, but for years? Or, if we speak of a blockade, are we ready to accept the implications of that for the Falkland Islanders now under the Argentine military occupation, or, I may say, for the large British community in Argentina? Are we ready to accept these considerations? It may be that we are, but I hope that we shall consider them carefully."

He was interrupted by another Conservative, Mr Alan Clark, who said: "My honourable friend has omitted to state that Argentina is a bankrupt totalitarian country, with an inflation rate of 130 per cent, and in an exceedingly precarious social condition. It has no capacity for replacing equipment that is destroyed. It has no capacity for buying, building or launching ships to replace those that are sunk. It has no capacity for replacing ammunition. Yet my honourable friend is talking as though this were a head-on confrontation with a world power."

So the debate continued. Sir Bernard Braine, MP for South-East Essex, said Britain had had "weasel words from successive Foreign Office Ministers over the Falklands and it was time for action . . . The very thought that our people, 1,800 people of British blood and bone, could be left in the hands of such criminals [Argentina's rulers] is enough to make any normal Englishman's blood – and the blood of Scotsmen and Welshmen – boil, too."

There were more attacks on the junta from Mr John Silkin, the Labour defence spokesman, when he wound up for the Opposition. He said President Galtieri was the worst of the bunch – a man who wore on his chest the medals he had won in repressing his own people, and he called him a "bargain basement Mussolini". Despite that, it was Mrs Thatcher, Lord Carrington and Mr Nott who were the "three most guilty people" in the government and were on trial.

The final speech of the debate came from Mr Nott. Political commentators to a man pointed out that he was a confident and nimble debater who had never had much trouble at the dispatch-box, but on this occasion his performance was disastrous.

His speech was repeatedly halted by Labour cries of "resign". He was howled down when he denied the government had been caught unprepared. There were roars when he said it would not have been right to take military action earlier. But he did say: "I do not seek to hide from Parliament the formidable difficulties with a crisis 8,000 miles away. However, the United Kingdom has the ability to mount a major naval task force and to sustain it for a period at that distance. The charge that the Royal Navy cannot do this is flagrantly and patently untrue. We have that capability, as will certainly be evident, and it amounts to a formidable force which no other nation in the world possesses with the exception of the Soviet Union and the United States."

The House was adjourned at two o'clock. It had correctly interpreted the mood of the country and its desire for firm action. Conservatives, Social Democrats and most Labour Party supporters had found themselves expressing unity of purpose, and in the England of the 1980s the voice of pacifism and appeasement was virtually stilled. The significance of this parliamentary debate was that it laid the foundations of purposeful solidarity which was to be so necessary as warlike preparations went ahead.

Even the most optimistic did not expect that such unanimity would last when the guns began to speak. In subsequent debates various factions began to express their doubts and fears. At least, though, the task force had the advantage of sailing out to liberate the Falkland Islands from Argentine rule secure in the knowledge that the nation as a whole was solidly behind it. Britain was about to embark on its most hazardous large-scale military enterprise since the end of the Second World War.

7

ARGENTINA'S INVASION OF SOUTH GEORGIA

Late on Friday, 2 April, news reached London that all British resistance on the Falkland Islands had ceased. Governor Rex Masterman Hunt, his wife and family had all been escorted to a Fokker of the Argentine Air Force which flew them from Stanley to Montevideo across the River Plate from Buenos Aires. The Royal Marines who had surrendered suffered the same fate and followed in an Argentine Hercules. From Montevideo they were repatriated to Britain.

But as Members of Parliament began assembling for the Saturday emergency debate in London, they were still unaware of what had happened in South Georgia. Earlier that same week, when attention was still concentrated on the apparently minor affair of the Argentine scrap dealers there, a detachment of twenty-two Royal Marines had been sent to the other island aboard HMS *Endurance*. She was ordered back to the Falklands after landing the Marines ashore. Lieutenant Keith Mills, the RM officer in command, had orders to keep a watching brief on the Argentine ice patrol vessel *Bahia Paraiso* which had been landing the stores and equipment at the port of Leith. Keeping most of his marines in Grytviken Lieutenant Mills dispatched a four-man squad to keep an eye on activities at Leith.

The British Antarctic Survey team of scientists was also still on the island. Indeed it was through them that the small force on South Georgia heard what was taking place in the Falklands. After Mills and the scientists had heard the Governor himself announcing that invasion of his islands was imminent, they stayed by the radio all night and eventually heard Governor Hunt put out his final message: "There is a landing craft coming through the narrows."

Lieutenant Mills, a capable twenty-two-year-old commando officer, made his own appreciation of the situation and began making his dispositions on the assumption that an attack was imminent and that the first target would be the survey team's base at Grytviken. He sent all the civilians to the old whaling station and they then took refuge in the white-painted wooden church. Convinced that he had a fair chance of holding any attack by the dozen or so Argentine Marines believed to be on board the *Bahia Paraiso*, Mills set about preparing his defences. On the most likely beach for an amphibious landing, the Marines improvised a minefield of oil drums filled with petrol and explosives, giant Molotov cocktails which could be detonated electrically. They also mined the wooden jetty and then began digging into a defensive position above the mined beach.

At five a.m. on Saturday morning, Mills' defensive calculations were badly upset by a report, from the boat crew which had gone to recover the four-man detachment posted at Leith, that the ice patrol ship had reappeared offshore and was now accompanied by an Argentine corvette.

"This threw a new light on things altogether," the Lieutenant reported later. "Now they had not just fifty or sixty Marines, but a ship capable of blasting us off the face of the island from a distance of several miles. But they would still have to land, and when they did I knew we could knock their numbers down, and give ourselves a fighting chance."

Now that the opposition was known to be much stronger than anticipated, Mills made plans to withdraw from his defensive position if it seemed likely to be overwhelmed. They would pull back from the beach and make for the mountains, from where they could harass the invaders, guerrilla style. A route was prepared and the Marines hid survival kits on a crevasse along it.

Lieutenant Mills was acting entirely on his own initiative until early Saturday morning, when he received a radio signal, presumably from the Ministry of Defence in London, by way of HMS *Endurance*. The twenty-two Royal Marines were expected to fight and not to surrender unless forced to. For this reason he doubted the truth of a radio message at ten forty-five from a man speaking English aboard the *Bahia Paraiso* claiming that Governor Hunt had surrendered the Falklands and all their dependencies which included South Georgia. The message was taken by Steven Martin, a civilian leader of the British Antarctic Survey, who replied that he needed time to consult. The Argentinians gave him five minutes. When Martin, who was stalling for time, suggested that the senior officer on the Argentine ship should come ashore for discussions, they demanded that everyone should line up on the beach so that they could be counted. "Then we are going to land some Marines to take over the island," said the officer on the warship. Asked whether he meant to take the island by force, he replied, "Yes, we do."

It was at this point that an Argentine Alouette helicopter appeared out of a clear sky. Confident that he had his men well placed in slit trenches supported by a machine-gun position up the cliff, Lieutenant Mills still thought it possible that the Argentines would put an officer ashore for talks before anything happened. So he walked towards the jetty, keeping an eye on the warship, until he suddenly spotted a second helicopter. It was landing troops only fifty yards away and, although he made a last diplomatic gesture of raising one hand as though to halt them, it was clearly too late for negotiations.

"Unless I was very careful I decided that I was going to end up with a 7.62 between my eyes," said Mills afterwards. Prudently he hit the deck and worked his way through dead ground back to the main position as the Argentines opened fire.

At this moment a Puma helicopter, which normally carries twenty-two men, zoomed in as though to land only a hundred yards from the Royal Marines' position. "Fire!" shouted Lieutenant Mills, and his Marines opened up with their two medium machine-guns, two light LMGs, automatic rifles and anti-tank rockets. They must have put at least five hundred rounds of small arms fire into the machine which pulled up quickly, with black smoke pouring from it. It skimmed heavily across the bay and dropped out of sight into a hollow.

The Marines then turned their fire upon two Alouette 3 helicopters which had begun landing troops on the other side of the bay and shot one of them down. But by this time Argentine troops on the ground were machine-gunning the British position and, even worse, the corvette began its bombardment. Its main armament consisted of a 40mm gun aft and a 100mm gun forward, and soon shells were exploding in the scree around the British position as bullets whined and screeched among the stones. Sergeant Peter Leach, a thirty-eight-year-old who had seen action in Malaya and Indonesia said later he had never experienced anything like this.

Fortunately for the defenders, the Captain of the corvette made a bad mistake at this point by bringing his ship right into the narrow bay of Grytviken, where once committed he would have to turn in a confined space. Mills realised this and waited until the range to the ship closed to a mere 300 yards. Then he shouted, "Right. Hit it," and the entire Marine detachment opened up. Their heaviest weapon was an 84mm Carl Gustav recoilless gun designed as an anti-tank weapon, and this action demonstrated for the first time that it could also be a useful weapon against ships. The first round landed thirty feet short of the target, but sped on like a skimming stone to smash into the corvette's hull with a tremendous explosion. Two smaller projectiles from a 66mm launcher also went home, as the ship was raked with small arms fire.

While the ship turned and began making speed out of the bay, a second Carl Gustav round hit into Exocet missile casings in place on the deck. Fortunately for the Argentine sailors the missiles did not explode, for had they done so the ship would have been blown to pieces.

Although his men were fighting well Lieutenant Mills

realised that it was only a question of time before they were
overwhelmed by superior numbers. The corvette now stood
offshore 3,000 metres away and, though handicapped by the
Marine's fire, she methodically began shelling the position
for a safe distance. The surviving helicopter had worked
round and landed Argentine troops, who moved to the flank
and cut off the Marines' escape route. Their young commander decided that he could accomplish nothing by fighting on
at the risk of heavy casualties. So far only one man, Corporal
Nigel Peters, had been injured.

"I just had to hope for the best," said Mills later. "It was a
bad moment. When I did get up, I took care to move very
gently."

Already he had hoisted an improvised white flag, the white
lining of some combat gear. As he approached the Argentines, he laid down his sub-machine gun. "Stop. Hands up,"
cried their officer. With as much dignity as he could muster,
the Commando Lieutenant explained that his aim had been
to force the Argentines to take military action in order to seize
the island. He had done that demonstrably and now proposed to surrender. Then he called his men forward by name
and, leaving their weapons behind them, they came slowly
down to be searched. The only moment of satisfaction for the
Marines, who had been in action for over two hours, came
when the Argentine officer asked incredulously, "Where are
all the rest? There must be at least fifty."

Together with the Survey people the RM detachment were
taken aboard the Argentine ice breaker under heavy guard
before being repatriated to Britain. They had fought well and
were fortunate not to have suffered heavier casualties than
just one injured NCO. The action also revealed that the
Argentines too intended to conduct operations according to
the rules, showing no desire for revenge, even though their
soldiers had been killed and some equipment destroyed.

When news of the brave action fought by Lieutenant Mills
and his twenty-one NCOs and Marines reached London, it
was the one cheering item in a weekend of unrelieved gloom,
helping considerably to alleviate the public disquiet brought

on by newspaper pictures of the other Marines at Stanley after they had surrendered. There they were disarmed, lying face downwards in their commando gear and guarded by Argentine soldiers. People did not blame the soldiers who had done their best, but the politicians, who had failed to make sure that the defences were strong enough.

For the first time since 1940, when German troops occupied the Channel Islands, British people – in this case the loyal Falklanders – found themselves under the military occupation of a foreign power. Humiliation was not the word to describe feelings at that stage. A more immediate worry predominated; if, after spending so much money on defence programmes, the British government was unable to protect its citizens (albeit at a range of 8,000 miles) from a third-rank power of invaders, how could it be ensured that the government would defend even the British Isles against any attack from such a power as the Soviet Union. A sense of danger – and reality – was in the air.

This was the mood which helps to explain the initial enthusiasm for the use of military and naval force to build up pressure on the Argentines to get out of the territory they had seized. Almost overnight it could be observed that Britain was transforming itself from a welfare state into a warfare state, not for glory, not for conquest and certainly not for economic gain, but in search of older values, and to prove that this particular political animal is dangerous. When attacked it is ready to defend itself.

For years, successive Labour and Conservative governments had been making defence cuts and reducing the strength of the Royal Navy even at a time when the Soviet Navy was greatly expanding. (Keith Speed, a Tory MP who was a minister concerned with the Navy, resigned in 1980 to draw attention to the dangers of a naval run down, but his was a lone voice.) So, when it became necessary to assemble a task force for the Argentine crisis, it came as almost a surprise that there were enough ships available for the enterprise. Fortunately the *Invincible* had not yet been delivered to her Australian buyers. Happily the *Hermes*, an old lady of the sea, was still available, even though, as a retired Captain commented as he watched her sail from Portsmouth, her rusty paintwork was by no means up to the standard he expected.

8

THE FOREIGN OFFICE AND
THE UNITED NATIONS

The first civilian casualties of the Falklands conflict were of a
political nature. They came about as a result of attacks on
Mrs Thatcher's government over the handling of the Argentine threat. Criticism came from the Labour Opposition,
from the Social Democrat/Liberal alliance and even from
indignant Tories. The complaints which they voiced were
those of the British people, namely that only government
blunders could have allowed the Argentines to sail into the
Falklands unopposed. There were angry demands for
vengeance not only against President Galtieri but against the
British government.

In the intemperate Saturday emergency debate, when Mr
John Silkin wound up for the Opposition he put the matter
squarely. "I say to the Foreign Secretary, the Defence Secretary and the Prime Minister the sooner you get out the
better." And the House of Commons echoed with cries of
"Resign. Resign." Of the three ministers named only Lord
Carrington, the Foreign Secretary, insisted that he must
resign. The Prime Minister, who was reluctant to lose the
services of so loyal and hitherto successful a minister, spent
most of Sunday trying to persuade him to change his mind.
But he maintained that it was his duty to go, and the two
senior ministers at the Foreign Office most concerned in the
affair, Humphrey Atkins and Richard Luce accompanied
him into the political wilderness.

Lord Carrington was a loss to the government, a minister
widely liked, loyal and effective. Since becoming Foreign

Secretary in May 1979 he had earned a reputation for
pragmatism and common sense among diplomats at home
and abroad. He had always wanted to be Foreign Secretary,
and that seems to have been the limit of his political ambition. When asked a question about whether he would like to
become Prime Minister which began, "Suppose Mrs
Thatcher were run over by a bus?" he replied firmly: "It
wouldn't dare!"

Lord Carrington, after tough and shrewd negotiations,
finally achieved the Rhodesian settlement to rid the British
government of a very awkward problem. As a result he came
to be thought of in Africa and to a certain extent in the
Middle East, where he also tried his best in the role of peace-
maker, as something of a miracle worker. Mrs Thatcher
was most unwilling to lose his powerful support and
experience in the new crisis. But Lord Carrington refused to
be persuaded that he could stay on with honour.

John Nott, the Defence Secretary, also offered to resign but
in his case Mrs Thatcher stood firm and insisted that he
should stay in office to get on with the job of preparing the
armed forces for action. In fact it was only reasonable that
the Foreign Office and its minister should have borne the
brunt of blame for what had happened. It was the department responsible for foreign intelligence, for examining and
for assessing the threat of Argentine moves which had begun
in late March. In this case the Defence Ministry was simply
the executive arm of foreign policy to take measures dictated
by Foreign Office decisions. Indeed by the time that Mr Nott
offered his resignation there was every indication that the
Defence Ministry was showing signs of remarkable efficiency
in mobilising the Royal Navy.

In general terms three main complaints were levelled at
the government: that it had failed to make a correct appreciation of the danger of an Argentine invasion; that its handling
of the scrap merchant incident was indecisive; and that it had
failed to keep Parliament properly informed. There were also
complaints that its whole defence policy had been a failure, in
that warships were not available swiftly enough to prevent a

fullscale invasion and crisis from taking place.

In the words of Michael Foot, the Opposition leader, who uncharacteristically was demanding deeds not words: "It seems that the British government has been fooled by the way in which the Argentine has gone about its business." Mr James Callaghan, the former Labour Prime Minister, had earlier recalled that on a previous occasion when the Argentines made threatening noises about a similar invasion plan, Royal Navy warships had been assembled in time, and without fuss had stood 400 miles off the Falklands to give support to the solitary HMS *Endurance* on the spot. That had been enough to prevent further action from Argentina.

Both the *Daily Telegraph* and *The Times* quoted "unimpeachable sources" of stories claiming that as early as 27 March information had been passed to the British government that an invasion plan was being launched, yet nothing had been done. It seemed certain that the Foreign Office had shown a lack of sensitivity to developments in the South Atlantic. Of course, it is in the nature of diplomats to favour appeasement rather than confrontation and the Foreign Office stuck to its story that the government had been advised not to use the Navy in case such a gesture upset diplomatic negotiations. In a speech celebrating the 200th anniversary of the formation of the Foreign Office, Lord Carrington had declared only a few weeks before: "We have far more influence and opportunity to exercise influence than the bare statistics of military and economic strength would suggest." It was a comment which gave insight into Foreign Office philosophy. It was perhaps one of his disadvantages as Foreign Secretary that because of his hereditary title this rather "whiggish" Tory sat in the House of Lords and was therefore not subject to the more intense probing of policies practised in the House of Commons.

There also remains a deep suspicion that behind the unwillingness to take the Argentine threats seriously at this time was Mrs Thatcher's constant obsession with the economy. To send units of the fleet would have cost money at a time when the government was trying to cut down expenditure in every field. Perhaps it seemed that the Falkland Islands were not worth the expense involved. If so, it was a bad miscalculation, for the subsequent operations on a very much larger scale have cost a great deal more.

In his letter of resignation Lord Carrington said he thought that much of the criticism of government policies was unfounded, but he was responsible for the conduct of that policy in foreign affairs and he thought it right to resign. In words which went right to the heart of the matter, he said: "The fact remains that the invasion of the Falkland Islands has been a humiliating affront to this country."

His resignation was deeply felt at the Foreign Office where Carrington was a popular minister, well liked for his easy aristocratic manner and sharp tongue. Nicholas Fenn, the chief spokesman, was almost in tears when he announced it, with the aim of making it absolutely clear that this was a Foreign Office matter not to be made public by a Downing Street spokesman. Both he and many other diplomats regarded Lord Carrington as the best Foreign Secretary for years. Lord Carrington's last act was to give a rather sad interview to Panorama on BBC television. It was typical of his style that he told Robert Kee, his interviewer, that in his present situation he could afford to stick out his tongue if he did not like a question. He repeated that he had resigned because of the great national humiliation, but produced a rather convoluted defence of his actions by declaring that the Foreign Office had not been wrong, given the information available about Argentine intentions. After all, they had been threatening military action to recover the Falklands for the last twenty years.

He strongly denied "taking his eye off the ball" because he was too occupied with other matters, though he did admit candidly that he had not got around to answering an Argentine message sent at the beginning of March which asked for a speeding up of talks. "But it is quite impossible for a Foreign Secretary who has all sorts of problems, the [EEC] Mandate, East–West relations, Poland, Namibia, all the rest of it, to sit down twenty-four hours a day in London and never leave his desk and talk about the Falkland Islands. I really do think people ought to keep a sense of proportion about it. There's a whole lot of people in the Office here who actually do look after the Falkland Islands."

Kee: "There was a Falkland Islands desk, looking after the Falklands problem all the time?"

Lord Carrington: "Of course."

Kee: "All the more reason surely they should have found out what was about to happen."

Lord Carrington: "You see, we're back where we were. We knew what the assessment was. It read that the assessments were different."

Kee: "Except that you got it wrong?"

Lord Carrington: "Well, what we got wrong was that the Argentines invaded . . ."

At the end of the interview a press photographer asked him: "Can we have one last picture of you sitting behind your desk in the Foreign Office?"

Making his way to the door, Lord Carrington paused, looked round the room, smiled and said: "I have no desk at the Foreign Office."

That desk was promptly taken over by Francis Pym, with twenty-one years' service in the House of Commons, a professional Tory politician, small and plump with smoothed-down hair and a gruff voice. He was very different in style to the rather elegant and amusing Lord Carrington to whom he paid tribute as a "very fine Foreign Secretary". His air of indifference concealed a political mind sharpened by spells of duty as Chief Whip, Secretary for Ulster, Shadow Foreign Secretary, Defence Secretary and, most recently, Leader of the House. A descendant of one of the great Parliamentarians, John Pym, who defied King Charles I he had been involved three times in disputes over the policies of Mrs Thatcher. At the Defence Ministry he refused to accept severe cuts in spending. He was replaced at that stage by the present Defence Secretary, Mr Nott, who had been put in to keep a firm hand on the purse strings of the armed services. But, by his stand, Mr Pym had won the loyalty of Conservative backbenchers and the admiration of service chiefs.

While the new man at the Foreign Office was having a late-night briefing from senior experts, Mrs Thatcher was trying to restore public confidence with a strong assurance that she would not even contemplate failure. When an interviewer asked her what the failure of naval operations would mean for her and for the future of her government, she was ready with an appropriate historical quote: "Do you remember what Queen Victoria said? 'Failure – the possibility does not exist.'"

With the disappearance of Lord Carrington, the strident demands that the men responsible for the debacle should be named and punished faded away, as politicians concentrated on what would happen next. However it was apparent that those hostile to Mrs Thatcher and her government were simply biding their time, waiting on events to see how successful she would be in coping with the crisis as it developed.

Meanwhile two Select Committees of MPs were set up to conduct enquiries. One involved the Defence Committee with the task of investigating "the state of readiness of Her Majesty's Forces in relation to the situation of the Falkland Islands and the dispositions which were made in the period of April 1982". The House of Commons Foreign Affairs Committee was regarded as a more serious threat to the Foreign Office, for its brief was to enquire into "the matters that led up to the invasion of the Falkland Islands and matters related thereto". This enquiry was to start at an appropriate moment, and it was assumed that it might not get down to business until the crisis had eased. If need be the two committees might work together. Some hearings will be held in secret session and ministers may be summoned to give evidence. In these circumstances it seems certain that a full investigation into the causes of the crisis will be made in the future.

It was just at the time that Lord Carrington was leaving office that the Foreign Office was working its hardest. Its task was not only to retrieve its damaged reputation but also to establish a solid base for further British diplomacy. The first notable success was at the United Nations, where Sir Anthony Parsons asked for a meeting of the Security Council.

After determined lobbying and a two-day battle of words, the Security Council passed Resolution 502 on Saturday, 3 April. This ordered cessation of all hostilities, the withdrawal of all Argentine forces from the Falklands and called upon Argentina and Britain to seek a diplomatic solution to their differences and to respect fully the purposes and principles of the United Nations Charter.

The voting pattern was interesting and gave great encouragement to the British government. Ten members of the Council voted for it and only one was against – the Central American state of Panama. The four abstainers were the Soviet Union, Poland (no doubt on orders from Moscow), China and Spain, which for reasons of Latin solidarity and remembering its continuing dispute over Gibraltar, could not bring itself to support the British. The ten in favour, including of course Britain herself, also comprised the United States, France, Ireland, Japan, Zaire, Togo, Uganda, Guyana and Jordan. The fact that countries representing such a wide political spectrum had supported the British case gave great strength to the British government and Resolution 502 became the bedrock on which all further action, both military and diplomatic, was firmly based.

The reference to the UN Charter was particularly valuable because Article 51 of that charter gives to all members the right to act in self-defence. The United Nations had always recognised Britain as the administrative power in the Falklands despite numerous challenges from Argentina, starting in 1965.

Naturally Senor Eduardo Roco, the Argentine Ambassador at the UN fought staunchly against Resolution 502 and described 150 years of British aggression against his country. He was ably backed up by his Foreign Minister, the mildsounding Nicanor Costa Mendez, who directed his undoubted talent for persuasion towards the non-aligned nations on the Council, urging them not to forsake a fellow

member of the club. Oleg Troyanovsky, the Soviet Ambassador, rallied to the Argentine cause by blaming Britain for
"stubbornly opposing decolonisation of the islands". Despite
that, the Soviet Union was unwilling to go the whole way in
voting for Argentina, nor did it veto the Resolution.

There was no doubt that Resolution 502 was a diplomatic
victory for Mrs Thatcher and it opened the way for requests
for support from fellow members of the European Community and from the United States. Already loyal members of the
old Commonwealth, such as New Zealand and Australia,
were rallying to the cause, and they were followed by the
Commonwealth organisation itself.

9

THE HAIG MISSION

Roars of laughter greeted the first mention of the Argentine invasion of the Falklands when questions were asked at the White House briefing in Washington on Monday, 5 April. To the smart press corps and the Californians who control the administration of President Ronald Reagan it all seemed too absurd to worry about. It was difficult for them to decide which was most absurd; an army of Latin American gauchos making a seaborne assault upon some small islands in the South Atlantic, of which they knew little, and which were ruled over by a British Governor in a cocked hat and uniform; or an England they considered a rather quaint tourist attraction, lovable, but old fashioned, assembling a task force to sail across the Atlantic to liberate those small islands.

But it was not long before the laughing had to stop. President Reagan realised here was a threat to his hemispheric policy. As we have seen he had telephoned President Galtieri in an unsuccessful attempt to prevent the invasion. The President was well aware of the realities. Mrs Thatcher's economic policies were similar to his own, and he was grateful for the diplomatic and practical support of Britain as a reliable ally.

On the other hand, he had been intending to rehabilitate Argentina after President Carter had ostracised the regime on moral grounds for its appalling record on human rights. If President Galtieri was prepared to go on putting his house in order, Argentina (not without liberal traditions despite the rule of a military junta) might become a very useful ally in a troubled continent. What the administration had to consider

among all its other great responsibilities around the world
was how to prevent "the spread of Cubas" in the neighbouring continent. Among the more respectable regimes allied to
America an anti-communist concensus was needed to build
the defences against Soviet influence, and against the influence of Kremlin surrogates. The very last thing President
Reagan wanted was a war between a staunch European ally
and a prospectively useful partner on his side of the Atlantic.

"Thank God that at least we have two weeks before the
British task force arrives to try to head off a disaster", was the
reaction of one Washington official. The administration
began using that time in hand with promptitude. President
Reagan at once denounced the invasion and called upon
Argentine troops to leave the Falklands, throwing the weight
of the American vote behind Britain in the UN Security
Council. But in order to give an appearance of neutrality,
necessary if the US was to set up as a diplomatic intermedi-
ary, officials cautiously began referring to "The Islands" so
as to avoid using the emotive names Falklands or *Malvinas*,
rather in the way that we have all agreed to speak of "The
Gulf", so as to offend neither Persians nor Arabs.

Both the Foreign Office and the British Embassy in
Washington were annoyed that Mrs Jeane Kirkpatrick, the
outspoken US representative at the United Nations, had
attended a dinner in her honour at the Argentine Embassy in
Washington a few hours after the invasion of the Falklands.
Sir Nicholas Henderson reproved her for this gesture,
shrewdly saying that it was as though he had gone to a dinner
at the Iranian Embassy the day the American hostages were
seized. This was a false analogy, snapped back the spirited
Mrs Kirkpatrick on television, and then compounded the
offence in her explanations by saying, "Now, if the Argentines own the islands, then moving troops into them is not
armed aggression."

Mr Reagan had already suggested in his telephone talk
with President Galtieri that he might send Vice President
George Bush, or "somebody like that", as a mediator. But
the Argentines were not responsive. As the crisis deepened, it

was Mr Alexander Haig, the US Secretary of State, who put himself forward as a go-between in the course of separate meetings with Sir Nicholas Henderson and Esteban Takacs, the Argentine Ambassador. This was the preliminary move which began the Haig mission during which the Secretary of State shuttled between Washington, London and Buenos Aires, clocking up some 26,000 air miles and heaven knows how many flying hours in nine days.

Alexander Meigs Haig, a sprightly fifty-eight-year-old retired general with a distinguished military record and long experience of government and of handling the bureaucracy, has been described as America's most political general since MacArthur. He learned the arts of diplomatic negotiation as the military assistant to Dr Henry Kissinger, the master of shuttle diplomacy. Dr Kissinger has spoken of him as: "strong in crises, decisive in judgment, skilful in bureaucratic infighting, indefatigable in his labours."

He wanted the task of trying to bring together Britain and Argentina because he believed important issues were at stake, but also because he is a man of great ambition, and this was to be the first great mission of this kind over which he had been given complete control. He was to report directly to the President himself.

Mr Haig had become Secretary of State at the end of a remarkable military career which began at West Point military academy and ended as Supreme Allied Commander, Europe. He brought with him to the State Department the sharp language of the barracks. If leaked reports of his remarks are to be believed, he not only called Lord Carrington "a duplicitous bastard", but also declared that "the British are lying through their teeth" over the international force in Sinai. Such may not be the language of true diplomacy, but for all that Mr Haig is seen as a reasonable and forceful man, and if anyone could have succeeded in this extremely tricky mission, he was the man. The British were happy to have him acting as an honest broker, well aware that his more right-wing opponents in the United States considered him to be "soft" on Europeans.

The start of the mission was delayed by half a day while a minor bureaucratic skirmish was settled in Washington. President Reagan and his court were off for a working holiday in Barbados to launch a new policy line there and it appears that this journey had taxed the aircraft resources of the White House. The Air Force Boeing placed at Mr Haig's disposal had no windows, nor were its communications adequate and he protested strongly. However the Secretary arrived in London looking spruce in a smart chalk-stripe suit, a British-looking trench coat and an Irish tweed hat – suitable attire for a soldier whose father was Scottish Presbyterian and whose mother was Irish Catholic, and who is a distant kinsman of Field Marshal Lord Haig, the British commander in the First World War. He had come as a listener and as a messenger and he made it clear that he had not packed in his travelling wardrobe any cut or dried American plan to resolve the dispute.

Mr Haig was a welcome visitor but Mrs Thatcher, while emphasising Britain's position as the closest ally of the United States, made it perfectly clear that she refused to concede sovereignty of the Falklands in return for vague concessions. There were five hours of talks in Downing Street followed by a steak dinner. Mrs Thatcher was also setting the pace, for the government had already announced that it intended to enforce the 200 mile exclusion zone around the Falklands. The country was prepared to go to war in forty-eight hours in order to make the point. The US Secretary of State listened carefully though no word of his comments emerged from Downing Street, which is more leak-proof than the White House. Then he returned to his Boeing, Air Force Three, as it was now called, and made the eighteen-hour flight to Buenos Aires.

A great crowd demonstration of noisy patriotism, planned to prove the unity of Argentines, had been organised to impress the North American visitor as he began a series of meetings with President Galtieri and the officers of his junta. The square outside Casa Rosada where the meetings were held was a sea of pale blue and white, the national colours of

Argentina. Two hundred thousand people waved their banners and sang patriotic songs. Among the more eye-catching
of them were ones bearing such slogans as, "Death to
Margaret's Swine", and "Goodbye Queen, God Save Argentina".

The feelings may have been genuine but the occasion was
carefully contrived to impress Mr Haig who had to leave the
conference place by helicopter in order to avoid the crowds.
After his departure President Galtieri appeared on the bal-
cony to declare that Argentina "was ready to teach a lesson
to anyone who dares touch a single metre of Argentine
territory. If the British want to come, let them come! We will
do battle." It was all done in the Peron tradition, a mixture of
threats and high-flown appeals to reason, such as, "I ask the
government and people of Britain for moderation. The nation must be prepared to extend its hand in peace, in a
gentlemanly and honourable way." Then the appeal was
followed by a straight statement: "The dignity and honour of
the Argentine nation is not negotiable by anyone."

What Mr Haig made of all this, he did not reveal, but it
must have convinced him that his shuttle diplomacy would
not easily succeed in reconciling two such determined leaders. He had eleven hours of talks with the Argentine leaders,
who took as firm a line in private as they did in public. Before
getting aboard Air Force Three for the second visit to
London, Mr Haig would only say that a lot of work had been
done and that he had some specific ideas for discussion. He
was increasingly aware that as he had linked his personal
reputation with achieving some success, a final effort would
be needed to try to bring the two sides closer.

Mr Haig also knew that pressure from the British side was
increasing hourly as the fleet approached the Falklands.
Back in London, and suffering from what was described as
"triple jet lag" and the fatigue of a man who only a few years
before had undergone heart by-pass surgery, he had several
more hours of talks with Mrs Thatcher and Mr Pym, the
Foreign Secretary.

Although the Argentines had taken notice of the British

warning not to send their warships into the 200 mile zone,
and had ordered their fleet back to home ports, the build-up
of their troops on the Falklands continued. Their nine C130
Hercules transports were airlifting soldiers and supplies into
the island, prompting Mr Haig to say "Time is slipping
away." He was able to talk over the telephone to Mr Costa
Mendez, the Argentine Foreign Secretary. The atmosphere
in Buenos Aires seemed calmer and more realistic after the
demonstrations, and newspapers there were beginning to
discuss the improving chances of negotiations. The telephone talk lasted half an hour and although details of its
content did not emerge, the feeling was that Argentina
seemed to be more amenable, even though it was not putting
forward any new proposals. The truth of the matter was that
Mr Costa Mendez was exercising his considerable diplomatic skills in an effort to prevent his country from taking the
blame for a breakdown of American diplomacy. He indicated
that the junta would be prepared to drop its previous insist-
ence on British recognition of Argentine sovereignty over the
islands before agreeing to withdraw its forces.

Mr Haig knew that this kind of statement was not enough
to convince the British government, nor could he be entirely
certain that such undertakings from the Foreign Minister
expressed the final will of the divided junta in Buenos Aires.
It was one of the strange features of all the negotiations that
the Argentine military government, widely considered to be
a dictatorship, was in fact a government constantly divided
and vacillating. The British government (a democratic form
of government which in the popular view leads to disunity
and divided views) was in fact unanimous and strong-
minded.

Nonetheless the US Secretary of State was determined
that there should be a negotiated settlement. He was well
aware of the importance of the issues involved and, taking a
world view, he warned both sides of the high stakes involved.
He knew that the Argentines considered him to be pro-
British, but he strove to keep a middle position, wearing a
brave face when he said in London that there had been

"some new ideas" from Buenos Aires. These ideas would
need further consideration, and he thought the time had
come to return to Washington and consult the President.

In the third-floor suite at the Churchill Hotel in London
Mr Haig's twenty-five aides and security staff once again
began loading their papers and the suitcases of the best
dressed Secretary of State. He had four suits with him, not to
mention his rackets and tennis gear. Once again they made
for London Airport in the bullet-proof limousines. Already
Mr Haig had out-shuttled Dr Kissinger, his tutor in personal
jetting diplomacy. He looked tired out but determined.

After a brief stay in Washington he made yet one more
journey to Buenos Aires in search of a settlement. "What is at
stake is so big that it demands a last effort by all those
involved," he said. At the airport he was greeted by Mr Costa
Mendez who had just declared on television that Britain was
over-reacting to the Argentine seizure of the Falklands.

By this time Mr Haig had put together a tentative five-
point peace plan. It called for the withdrawal of Argentine
troops from the Falklands in return for the departure of the
British task force; a provisional administration of the islands
by Britain, Argentina, and the United States until December
1982, after which date there would be fresh talks on future
relations between Argentina and the Falkland Islands. Procedures would be established for discovering the wishes of
the Falkland Islanders. There would be an early resump-
tion of air and communications links which had existed
between Stanley and the mainland before the invasion of
2 April.

Washington saw these proposals as a basis for negotiations. No mention was made of the fundamental and thorny
question of sovereignty. But Mr Haig believed that if consideration of that could be left until a later stage, then at least
some measure of agreement might be reached. It was the
same technique employed by American diplomacy in the
Israeli–Egyptian negotiations – to establish a momentum of
negotiation and to leave the most difficult part until the end.

For four days Mr Haig managed to keep talking with the

junta, escaping only on one occasion for a game of tennis with the US Ambassador. Things were not helped by another public declaration from President Galtieri that "the *Malvinas* are our islands and we are not going to abandon them."

It was not an easy time for negotiating and on occasion both the Americans and the Argentines spoke bluntly. At one stage Mr Haig slapped shut his files and warned: "If you don't accept, it will mean war." With equal force President Galtieri gathered up his papers and snapped: "If it's war, you Americans will also be responsible."

All that the Argentines had to offer was a proposal, unacceptable in London, that they would withdraw forces from the Falkland Islands in two stages on condition that the British removed their fleet in one stage. They also insisted on measures to allow large-scale settlement on the islands by Argentines, and the establishment there of a temporary administration shared between Britain and Argentina. The issue of sovereignty was to be negotiated under United Nations auspices within a limited period.

On Monday, 19 April, Mr Haig departed from Buenos Aires, talking bleakly about the dangers of war. In his command centre, aboard Air Force Three, he settled down into the twenty-foot curved sofa in the middle section of the aircraft and spoke on the telephone to London and to Washington. As he flew away from it all at 35,000 feet he must have known that, despite all his efforts, the mediation mission so far was a failure. The Argentines had not backed down. They had not agreed to obey Resolution 502 of the United Nations, ordering them to withdraw their forces. The British were in no mood to compromise, their task force was sailing ever closer to the Falklands and warlike preparations were in full swing.

Back in Washington the Secretary of State found little praise for all his efforts. Indeed he had become the victim of a whispering campaign from his critics, and the White House had to deny that he would resign if his peace efforts failed.

Ordinary Americans, and the politicians who represented them were beginning to express their feelings that the time had come for the United States to get off the fence of neutrality and come down on the side of Britain, their old ally across the Atlantic.

10

PREPARATION FOR ACTION

As the British battle fleet slipped out of Portsmouth harbour and steamed slowly down the misty Solent it seemed less menacing than the huge battleships of two world wars with their menacing sixteen-inch gun turrets. In comparison the tiny 4.5 inch single gun turrets and neat missiles of the modern ships gave them almost a toy-like appearance; only the Harriers on the decks of the carriers suggested the awesome firepower that this fleet carried. Few could ignore the irony behind the spectacle for many of these ships were up for sale or destined for the scrapyard, and were manned by sailors who were being paid off because of the defence cuts. Nevertheless, they made a brave sight and the crowds lining the shore waved their Union Jacks and cheered them on their way, as the most powerful fleet Britain has put to sea for over thirty years sailed past.

What was remarkable about the fleet's departure was the speed and efficiency with which it had been put together and turned into a formidable fighting force. Men were recalled from leave, including Prince Andrew who received a call at Buckingham Palace to report for duty as a helicopter co-pilot on HMS *Invincible*. Stores, weapons, aircraft, sailors and soldiers appeared on quaysides as if by magic. Somebody, somewhere had got it right.

More and more ships were added to the fleet. It was an uneven mixture. HMS *Hermes*, 28,700 tons, the veteran carrier which has been in service for twenty-three years, was named flagship. She was joined by the two-year-old *Invincible* of 19,500 tons, which used to be called a "through deck cruiser" but which is really a light aircraft carrier, and was

due to be sold to Australia, and HMS *Fearless*, the amphibious assault ship of 12,500 tons which had just been saved
from the breaker's yard. With them went destroyers, frigates
and supply vessels of the Royal Fleet Auxiliary. And they
were to be joined at sea by a larger group of frigates and
destroyers which had sailed from Gibraltar after taking part
in the annual exercise, Spring Train. Among them were the
two large County Class destroyers *Glamorgan* and *Antrim*;
three Type 42 destroyers, the ill-fated *Sheffield* and *Coventry*
and their sister ship the *Glasgow*; three Type 22 frigates,
Broadsword, *Battleaxe* and *Brilliant*; four Leander class frigates,
Dido, *Ariadne*, *Aurora* and *Euryalus*; and four Rothesay class
frigates, *Plymouth*, *Lowestoft*, *Yarmouth* and *Rhyl*. There were
also the nuclear-powered submarines and although the Defence Ministry, in an attempt to deter the Argentines from
invading, had been content to foster the story that HMS
Superb was travelling towards the Falklands at her full thirty
knots when she was in fact heading for her base in Scotland,
there is no doubt that other hunter-killers were dispatched to
the war zone.

At the same time the government started a crash programme of chartering, requisitioning and converting merchant vessels to carry troops and materiel to the Falklands
and to maintain a supply line some 8,000 miles long. Tankers, roll-on roll-off ferries, luxury liners were all pulled
into the seaborne supply train. The liners *Canberra* and
Queen Elizabeth II were taken over, fitted with helicopter
decks and turned into troopships. Disappointed holiday-
makers looking forward to "the cruise of a lifetime" were
turned away from the ships and given their money back. The
SS *Uganda*, which has taken so many thousands of schoolchildren on educational cruises, was turned into a hospital ship.

Lloyds of London said that all merchant ships requisitioned would continue to be covered by their insurance until
the position had been clarified by the government. In government service the state covers extraordinary risks such as a
ship being mined or torpedoed, but damage caused by the
negligence of the captain or crew could still be a matter for

civilian insurance. This was one of a number of awkward questions which were being settled as the ships were gathered. How much would their civilian crews be paid if they volunteered for service in the war zone? How much would the owners of the cruise liners be paid not only for the use of their ships but for compensation for loss of earning from their profitable cruises?

At the same time, the soldiers were being gathered, an initial thousand men of the Royal Marines, followed by two battalions of the Parachute Regiment and more Marines. Guns, Scorpion tanks and all the supporting arms needed by an invading force were loaded onto an astonishing variety of ships. And, most important of all, the Harriers, the jump jets which were to provide the only cover and strike force of the fleet. Twenty of them were crowded onto the *Invincible* and the *Hermes*, whose normal complement is five Harriers each. Twenty-two more Harriers, both Sea Harriers and the less sophisticated RAF strike version, were due to sail on the converted container ship *Atlantic Conveyor*. Some of these however, in a brilliant piece of airmanship, flew all the way to Ascension Island, refuelling in flight. Almost as important as the Harriers were the Sea King and Lynx helicopters to be used not only for ferrying assault troops but, armed with missiles and rockets and torpedoes, to provide a fearsome array of mobile firepower.

Command of the sharp end of this array of naval and military power was given to a new-style admiral, Rear Admiral John "Sandy" Woodward, a submariner who after a period in the Defence Ministry as Director of Naval Plans was appointed Flag Officer First Flotilla in August 1981. An unassuming Cornishman, he lives in Surbiton and although he gets his nickname from his red hair he does not stand out among the friends with whom he sails in his spare time. A collector of stamps and antiques, he is a brilliant mathematician but had never seen action before the Falklands. Talking to reporters with the task force he said: "I am very astonished to find myself in this position. I am an ordinary person who lives in South-West London, in suburbia. I have been a virtual civil servant for the past three years, commuting into London every day." However, he was soon to find himself in the midst of battle with the Argentines and under sharp criticism not only from the press but also from his superiors in the Service and Mr Michael Foot.

Overall command of the whole enterprise rested with Admiral Sir John Fieldhouse, Commander in Chief, Fleet, whose headquarters are "HMS *Warrior*", set among the mansions of the Middlesex stockbroker belt at Northwood. There, Sir John is master of the Queen's Navy. There are two office blocks, one for Sir John and one for his RAF counterpart. But the real headquarters, known as "the hole", is underground, part of it below what was once a croquet lawn. It has its own air, power and water supplies and can be sealed off by massive steel doors in the event of a nuclear attack.

In the "hole", each branch of naval warfare has its own "cell" with groups of officers dealing with submarines; air defence; mine counter-measures; intelligence, and communications and the centre of it all is the operations room, dominated by a huge wall chart on which different lights tell the positions of friendly and enemy ships and aircraft throughout the world. As with almost everything else in the Navy now this ops. room is run by computers. The "hole's" computers are linked to satellites and are in instant contact with Sandy Woodward via the *Invincible* which was fitted with a SCOT (Satellite Communications Terminal) before she sailed for the Falklands. And so, for the first time in the history of naval warfare the overall commander has been able to talk to the men actually fighting 8,000 miles away.

However, despite all this electronic wizardry, the power of the fleet and the professionalism and dedication of the soldiers it was carrying, grave doubts persisted about its chances of success in an attack on the Falklands. There was no doubt that the fleet would sweep the South Atlantic clear of Argentine ships. The enemy's fleet (led by the ancient aircraft carrier *Veinticinco de Mayo* which had started life thirty-nine years previously as HMS *Venerable* before it was sold to the Dutch who sold it in their turn to the Argentines,

and supported by the cruiser *General Belgrano*, which had
survived the Japanese attack on Pearl Harbor as the USS
Phoenix) had only two modern Type 42 *Sheffield* class destroyers and three modern French-built frigates to bolster its
collection of Second World War destroyers and diesel-
powered submarines. Despite the fact that most of the destroyers and frigates were armed with the French-built Exocet
missiles, the Argentine Navy was thought to be no match for
the task force, equipped with the nuclear-powered hunter-
killers, whose computerised Tigerfish torpedoes could sink
any ship that made a hostile move.

What gave the strategists pause for thought was the fact
that Argentina itself was an unsinkable aircraft carrier and
had a total of nearly two hundred war planes. Most of them
were ageing Skyhawks, but they had proved robust, reliable
attack bombers in the Middle East wars and it was known
that the Mirages and Israeli-built Daggers were potent
fighting aircraft while the Dassault Super Etendards and
their air-fired Exocets were an unknown quantity. All these,
even though they were operating at extreme range against
only twenty Harriers, made the odds somewhat more daunt-
ing and it was unacceptable that the troops should be put
ashore without securing air supremacy over the beaches. In
particular there was no wish to subject the assault forces to
the attentions of the Argentine-built Pucara ground attack
aircraft which proved their efficacy in the Argentine war
against the left-wing guerrillas. They carry two 30mm cannon, four 7.62 machine guns and a mixture of nearly 4,000
pounds of various bombs and rockets. So from the outset it
became obvious that the airport at Stanley would have to be
knocked out.

The other great problem which militated against success
was of course the enormously long line of communication
that stretched across 8,000 miles of sea into a South Atlantic
where winter, with its awesome storms, was approaching
fast. The difficulties of keeping the fleet supplied, of replacing
lost aircraft and keeping the men fit were obviously going to
be immense. The ideal forward base, Simonstown at the tip

of South Africa, which had been a Royal Navy haven for so many years had been given up for anti-apartheid reasons which may well have been justified but which left the Navy without a base except for the tiny speck of barren rock called Ascension Island. It covers thirty-four square miles and was uninhabited until Napoleon was sent to exile on neighbouring St Helena and British troops were stationed there.

It slumbered away until the Second World War, when the Americans built an air base there and called it Wideawake after the sea-bird which is the island's most numerous inhabitant. Thereafter it became an important communications centre and the Americans continued to lease the air base. However the leasing arrangement entitled Britain to use most of its facilities and we have maintained a small liaison office there. The BBC built a relay station in the mid-1960s and Cable and Wireless routes telephone and cables through the island and has built a communications satellite tracking station. Few of the island's 1,000 inhabitants had any idea how important this desolate rock was to become in a major military enterprise. The first indication of what was about to happen came on 6 April when the fleet auxiliary *Fort Austin*, a ship of 8,160 tons, arrived and began taking on stores. Then four RAF Hercules transports arrived on the airstrip, known locally as Miracle Mile, and Mr Bernard Pauncefort, the British administrator, announced that the airstrip would be restricted to authorised traffic.

The following day the Defence Secretary, Mr John Nott, told the House of Commons, to cheers from the Conservative benches, that as from four a.m. Greenwich Mean Time on 12 April, Easter Monday, a war zone would be imposed for 200 miles around the Falkland Islands and that any Argentine warships and naval auxiliaries found within the zone would be treated as hostile and would be liable to be attacked by British forces.

For the first time the world began to understand that Britain meant what it said and that it would use force to take back what had been stolen. Mr Nott, in a parliamentary performance which was markedly different from his abjectness of five days before, said: "We have no wish to shed blood but we will not acquiesce in an act of unprovoked aggression undertaken, presumably, in the false belief that we lack the courage and the will to respond. Let the world be under no illusion. These people are British. We mean to defend them. We are in earnest and no one should doubt our resolve."

Stirring words. The game was afoot.

11

THE ECONOMIC BATTLE

Britain's preparations to wage economic war against Argentina went hand in hand with her military preparations. All trade was halted, credit stopped and 1.4 billion dollars of Argentine assets held in London were frozen. This is about one quarter of their total reserves. It was understood well enough that sanctions alone never decide wars – they had not worked against Ian Smith's Rhodesia and they had no discernible effect on Russia's intervention in Afghanistan – but with a country whose economy was in such a parlous state as Argentina's they were bound to have some effect even if they were more a display of disapproval than measures which would bring the junta to heel. After all, the Argentines had lived with galloping inflation, a weak peso, a huge overseas debt and fifteen per cent unemployment for a number of years. Anything that sanctions could do in the short term would not make all that much difference to a country which had its own oil wells and more than enough meat and bread.

What was important however was that all military supplies and financing for buying weapons abroad should be cut off. This became even more important when the French built Super Etendard strike aircraft, mated with the Exocet missile, wrecked HMS *Sheffield*. France had still not supplied all the fourteen Super Etendards and their Exocets which had been ordered by the Argentines before they invaded the Falklands. It was essential for the safety of the British fleet that the rest should not get through.

Britain's European allies and the Commonwealth backed her imposition of sanctions with dramatic speed. France,

West Germany, Belgium and the Netherlands embargoed all arms sales. This meant a considerable sacrifice for Germany because Blohm and Voss were building four frigates and had contracted to supply equipment for six corvettes being built in Argentina. Germany could not prevent the Argentines continuing the construction of the corvettes but would not supply the equipment. A similar embargo was placed on equipment for four German-designed submarines being built under licence in Argentine shipyards.

This embargo was followed by a full ban on sales of arms by members of the Common Market. And, unexpectedly, Britain won comprehensive support for a total ban on Argentine imports by the members of the EEC. Norway, although not a member of the EEC, also banned Argentine imports. The EEC ban was estimated to effect up to thirty per cent of Argentina's export business, a severe blow to a country desperately short of foreign exchange. Argentina retaliated by banning imports from the EEC and while this move had little effect on the immediate situation it promised unpleasantness in the future.

Australia and Hong Kong stopped all Argentine imports. Canada halted the export of military hardware to Argentina, principally helicopter parts and replacement gear for armoured vehicles. New Zealand imposed sanctions and broke off diplomatic relations. Japan was equivocal, announcing that an "economic measure" would be instituted, but it amounted to no more than not taking advantage of the situation by increasing its trade with Argentina. Britain reacted by complaining that the Japanese position was disappointing and not "fully cooperative" as a member of the West. The Japanese were in fact caught in the middle because Buenos Aires was complaining at the same time that the Japanese did not fully appreciate the Argentine position on the Falklands issue. Nevertheless the Argentines were attacking the resolution of the less committed members of the EEC, threatening that Japan would replace the European countries in the post-Falklands trade line-up.

Britain had to wait until the Haig mission had failed before the United States could abandon its even-handed policy and announce economic and military sanctions against the junta in favour of Britain, "our closest ally". President Reagan decided on two specific measures:

1. Suspension of all military exports to Argentina, and the withholding of certification of Argentine eligibility for military sales.

2. Suspension of new export-import bank credits and guarantees, and the suspension of commodity credit corporation guarantees.

At the same time the Secretary of State, Mr Haig, announced that the Americans would "respond positively" to British requests for military materiel while making it plain that there would be "no direct US military involvement". However, it was noted that the United States did not place an embargo on trade with Argentina, which is currently running at 3 billion dollars a year, nor did it attempt to interfere with American private bank loans to Argentina. These loans, to the government and private companies, amount to more than 9 billion dollars.

It is in this respect that the economic war took on an importance outside the immediate conflict, for it was estimated that if Argentina defaulted on just one part of its vast 32 billion dollar international debt it could not only cost individual banks a great deal of hard cash but shake the whole system of international banking. Lloyds, National Westminster and the Midland all risk loss. According to Euromoney Syndication Guide, Lloyds is the agent bank for Argentinian loans for 1.2 billion dollars. The next largest is Morgan Guaranty of New York with just under 1 billion dollars. In all, nearly 6 billion dollars of Argentina's 32 billion dollars of foreign debt have been borrowed from banks in Britain of which nearly 2 billion is believed to be owed to the clearing banks themselves. These are awesome figures on their own but what was feared even more was the knock-on effect of an Argentinian default on the shaky economies of other South American states, up to their eyes in debt to the West. Just as the economic collapse of Poland could bring about a domino effect in Eastern Europe, so could the collapse of Argentina effect the rest of South America.

However, as the crisis continued, Argentina maintained its prompt repayments on its foreign debts – except of course to British banks. The junta obviously wanted to demonstrate its readiness to meet its foreign obligations. But how long could it maintain those payments? It had already admitted that it needed to borrow another 7 billion dollars this year just to service its debts and nobody, even outside the embargo countries, was particularly anxious to invest yet more money in a country tottering on the edge of bankruptcy.

As the sanctions began to bite, harsh economic measures were taken. The peso was devalued by seventeen per cent to the extraordinary rate of 14,000 to the dollar, reflecting the raging inflation of about 140 per cent now being boosted even higher by the extra burdens of financing the Falklands conflict. Two weeks after the Argentine Marines landed on the Falklands the conflict was estimated to have cost the regime up to 500 million dollars. The junta was doing all it could to raise money. It staged a music festival to raise pesos, gifts and morale. President Galtieri sold his beloved horse Fomento for 46 million pesos (about £1,800) and donated the proceeds to the *Malvinas* Patriotic Fund.

In this game of economic poker the Argentines seemed to have an ace in the unlikely form of the Soviet Union. The Russians first became important customers of Argentina in 1972, and trading links between the politically opposed countries have grown since the military seized power from Peron's widow in 1976. Successive Russian harvest failures in the last three years and the American embargo on grain sales because of Afghanistan brought even greater purchases of meat and grain until Argentina exported seventy-five per cent of its grain crop to the Soviet Union. This year alone the Russians agreed to purchase between 60,000 and 100,000 tonnes of beef. The trade balance is overwhelmingly in Argentina's favour. Last year Soviet exports to Argentina were worth 40 million dollars; imports from Argentina to-

talled a massive 3.3 billion dollars. The resulting deficit
accounts for eighty per cent of Moscow's hard currency debt.

And there's the rub for Argentina. Although the Soviet
Union might wish to ensure its supplies of meat and grain, it
does not have the foreign currency to go to the junta's aid. As
the conflict proceeded there was growing evidence that far
from helping the Argentines, Moscow was attempting to
profit from their troubles by cutting back on cereal purchases
in order to force down the price. Further trouble loomed for
Buenos Aires with the approach of the 24 May deadline, after
which Lloyds had declared they would no longer be responsible for the insurance cover of ships traversing the South
Atlantic war zone. This refusal of insurance cover threatened
grain shipments even more.

The only lightening of the economic situation for Argentina came when the month of sanctions agreed to by the EEC
ran out and was extended by only a week with a number of
the member nations beginning to insist on a negotiated
solution. Opposition to a renewal of the sanctions was led by
Ireland and Italy. The Irish Prime Minister, Mr Charles
Haughey, explaining his country's attitude, said that he had
reluctantly gone along with the sanctions originally on the
understanding that they were intended to support a diplomatic solution. When it became clear that they were in
support of military activity his government had to review its
position. "As a neutral country we cannot subscribe to the
use of sanctions in support of military action." The Italians
had a more pressing domestic reason for wanting to opt out.
Nearly fifty per cent of the Argentine population are of
Italian origin with close links to families in Italy and they
were putting a great deal of pressure on a shaky government
to withdraw its support for Britain.

The effect of the decision was to put Britain on probation
to seek a negotiated settlement or forfeit EEC support.
France and Germany, however, made it clear that they
would not withdraw their support, and the Italian and Irish
stand was criticised by many in their own countries.

There was an element of "linkage" in the vote because

Britain was engaged simultaneously in hard bargaining over
farm prices and the budget. Although this was denied there
was no doubt that Britain's desire for a renewal of sanctions
was used as a lever in the other debates. Britain's discom-
fiture therefore may have involved subtleties that were lost
on the junta. What it saw was a Britain rapidly losing
support among its European allies and the prospect that
trade, if not the supply of arms, might be resumed again
shortly.

In Britain itself, apart from the tight-lipped bankers (who
were seeking to safeguard their loans in the face of a possible
collapse of the Argentine economy), the City waited and
watched, swinging up and down with each round of negotiations, each burst of firing. As the possibility of a British
assault on the Falklands rose so prices on the Stock Market
plunged. On 17 May they fell 14.8 points, the largest one-day
fall in six months. But there was little panic. It was a question
of wait and see. For companies involved in defence work, it
was a case of "now thrive the armourers" and, although the
City insisted that their shares were doing well because of
expected profits from the previous year's trading, there was
no doubt that the success of British missiles in the South
Atlantic was doing them no harm at all.

One curiosity brought about by the conflict is that Argentina is still committed to pay Williams and Glyn's Bank £6
million, the final payment on the two Type 42 destroyers,
sister ships of the ill-fated *Sheffield*, which were built for the
Argentine Navy by Vickers. If Argentina were to renege on
the payment falling due in the first week of July, then the
bank would be able to claim the money from the Export
Credits Guarantee Department, the government's insurance
company. And what if the ships were sunk by the British task
force before the payment became due? War is full of such
ironies. Another is, of course, the mini-boom in the dockyards which were drifting into disuse and had to come alive
again to send out the fleet. Unless the government changes its
mind on its programme of defence cuts however, the run-
down of the naval dockyards will continue.

What remains to be seen is the effect of the conflict on Britain's long-term prospects of economic revival. At the outset the government imposed no limit on the amount of money to be spent on the military effort to repossess the Falklands. Mr Brittan, Chief Secretary to the Treasury, made it quite plain: "The needs of the task force must and will come first."

So, the economic battle lines were drawn just as were the military lines. Both sides were committed to spending whatever was necessary to maintain their military position. One side, classed as a "less developed country", deep in debt and starting out with most of its creditors ranged against it, its economy in a shambles and coming under increasing pressure as the casualty list of bills rolled in – its economic existence threatened. The other, a creditor, but itself engaged in a controversial monetary experiment designed to restore its economy to prosperity, and with support slipping away among some of its EEC partners, and its government arguing that it would not be thrown off its economic course by the added military expenditure.

As the decision on whether or not there would be a full-scale assault came to be taken it seemed possible that the economic war would be even more dangerous for both sides in the long run than its military counterpart.

12

THE INTELLIGENCE WAR

Military intelligence – the soldier's need to "see the other side of the hill", to know his enemy's strength and intentions – is vital in every war but never more so than in this conflict, a limited war hedged about by political restrictions but fought with the most modern weapons, in which one quick attack with a single missile had a political effect far greater than the physical damage it caused. The speed of modern missiles made it all the more important to obtain accurate information as quickly as possible. The British needed to know the radar frequencies of Argentina's missiles so that they could be confused by electronic counter measures. The Argentines needed to know the positions of the British ships so that they could estimate when and how an attack could develop.

It is intriguing therefore that in these days of "Elint", electronic intelligence, the first coup was acquired by old-fashioned espionage. British agents in Buenos Aires obtained details of the Argentine's invasion plans some two weeks before their fleet sailed for Stanley. But, as so often happens with such coups, it was given little credence because it did not fit in with the thinking of the men to whom it was reported.

No doubt those agents are still working away on Britain's behalf, but once the invasion became a fact – probably even before – the secret battle moved out of the traditional field and into the electronic age with the super powers America and Russia looking down from space, all-seeing, all-hearing, just as they did during the Yom Kippur War when Moscow and Washington knew more about the overall progress of the war than the commanders in the field.

The British immediately called on the United States to honour the agreements made between the two countries for the exchange of intelligence. In fact the two countries work so closely together in this field that much of their intelligence work is of a joint nature and the Americans willingly agreed to help. It is still not known however how far the Russians have gone in helping the Argentines. Certainly the Russians would like to keep the Argentines as cooperative business partners in order to ensure their supplies of Argentine grain and meat but that is an argument which cuts both ways and there remain deep ideological differences between the two countries. It could also prove embarrassing to the Soviet Union if she were shown to have helped a regime as bitterly anti-Communist as Argentina's.

Mr Norman Bailey, director of planning for America's National Security Council, said early on in the conflict that the Russians were providing intelligence to the Argentines on the movement of British forces but this was refuted by the junta, whose spokesman said: "Our interests with the Soviet Union are strictly commercial. We do not share any political or ideological alliance."

It would also be unwise for the Russians to give the Argentines detailed accounts of British activities because these reports could reveal secrets of Russia's own electronic espionage capabilities and there is no doubt that there are officers in the Argentine forces who are sufficiently anti-Communist to pass on such reports to the Americans. So the likelihood is that the Russians have given Argentina a certain amount of low-level information but nothing which could later prove to be either politically or militarily embarrassing.

What is certain is that the Russians have been following the course of the conflict with every means available to them. The *Primorye* class intelligence vessel, one of which is normally stationed between Scotland and Ireland to track the movements of British and American nuclear submarines operating out of Holy Loch, was dispatched to shadow the *Canberra* as she steamed to the war zone. These intelligence-gathering vessels are no longer converted fishing boats hung about with a few aerials but a proper naval class of vessel of 3,400 tons, and manned by a crew of 117, most of whom are expert technicians working on an array of radar, sonar and radio interception devices.

The Russians also brought their TU142 Bear maritime reconnaissance aircraft into operation. With a range of 7,000 miles, packed with electronic surveillance equipment, and flying out of the Cuban-operated military airfield near Luanda in Angola, these aircraft were able to dog the fleet's progress, not only reporting position and course but also listening in to radio traffic.

However, neither the Bears nor the *Primorye* vessel chose to challenge the total exclusion zone declared by the British in the battle area. Instead the Russians left their spying to their satellites. In a flurry of launches dating from two days before the invasion, the Soviets put up no less than eight Cosmos satellites in orbits which enabled them to look down on the Falklands area. On 31 March they launched Cosmos 1345, designed to pick up radar transmissions from ships, and Cosmos 1347 which listens in to sea and air communications in a funnel-shaped area below its orbit. On 2 April Cosmos 1347 was put into orbit over the Falklands. Its role is photographic reconnaissance, and it ejects its film capsules as it passes over Russia. Two more high-resolution photographic satellites, Cosmos 1350 and Cosmos 1353 were launched on 16 April and 23 April. Cosmos 1351, another radar-sensing device, was launched on 21 April, presumably to take over the task of the withdrawn Bears as the task force sailed into the South Atlantic. On the same day another photographic satellite, Cosmos 1352, was put into orbit. And then, on 28 April, they sent up another electronic eavesdropping satellite, Cosmos 1354. An even more sophisticated satellite was launched on 15 May. Equipped with a nuclear-powered radar unit which enables the satellite to "see" through cloud, the Russians put it into an orbit passing directly over the Falklands.

All these spies in the sky provide the Soviet Union with

both an overall and detailed picture of the battle zone and the combatants. What is not known is whether they are able to break the "short-time" codes which are electronically scrambled in a random pattern and are used in fleet communications. The Navy has grown used to Soviet spying over the years and takes a fairly relaxed view of it. It is all a question of knowing when a satellite is due overhead and keeping silent until it swings over the horizon or, as one spokesman put it: "We are well experienced in minimising the amount of intelligence that the Russians can collect and we are putting that experience to good use. Satellites can only be in one place in the sky at one time." Also, with the weather conditions which prevail in the South Atlantic, the photographic satellites were taking splendid photographs of clouds, but little else. Perhaps that is the reason the weather in the area was declared a military secret. It cannot have had anything to do with the Argentines because they are fully aware of their own weather. Nevertheless, with the Russians spending immense amounts of money and material in putting virtually a squadron of spy satellites into space, the amount of intelligence they gathered had to be considerable. The question remains: How much and of what grade have they passed to the Argentines?

There can be no doubt of the extent of the help given by the Americans to Britain. When Mr Haig was engaged in his attempt to settle the conflict, he became angry at stories that US intelligence was being passed to Britain. His anger was understandable because the reports undermined his position as an honest broker and before he flew to Buenos Aires he said: "Since the onset of the crisis the United States has not acceded to requests that would go beyond the scope of customary patterns of cooperation based on existing bilateral agreements." All true. But those "existing bilateral agreements" are strong and extensive. Similarly, when Mr Norman Bailey was asked if the US had ordered its SR71 Blackbird reconnaissance planes to fly missions over the Falklands area, he replied: "Yes, but not to aid the British." The fact of the matter was that although the flights were

Port Stanley Harbour, before the invasion *(The Falkland Islands Office)*

Rex Hunt, Governor of the Falklands, wearing his official uniform and putting on a brave face after the surrender *(Daily Telegraph/Ken Clarke)*

The disused whaling station on South Georgia where the dispute began *(Associated Press)*

The British surrender: 2nd April 1982
(Camera Press/Ken Clarke)

The British Marines are relieved of their arms by their Argentine captors *(Daily Telegraph/Ken Clarke)*

Argentine troops on the march in the Falklands: 28th April 1982 *(Associated Press)*

The Argentine Marine Corps patrol the streets of Port Stanley, in an amphibious personnel carrier

(Associated Press)

A *Kelper* waves a white flag of truce as she walks past an Argentine soldier in Port Stanley

(Daily Telegraph/Ken Clarke)

Top left: The Argentine Foreign Minister, Nicanor Costa Mendez *(Associated Press)*

Top right: The Argentine President, Leopoldo Galtieri *(Associated Press)*

Left: General Mario Menendez takes the oath as the Governor of the *Islas Malvinas (Associated Press)*

British Foreign Secretary, Lord Carrington: he resigned on 5th April 1982
(Camera Press)

Prime Minister Mrs. Thatcher with U.S. Secretary of State Alexander Haig and, right, Britain's new Foreign Secretary, Francis Pym, on 8th April 1982
(Associated Press)

The Commander-in-Chief of the British Task Force, Rear Admiral John F. Woodward *(Camera Press)*

H.R.H. Prince Andrew, Acting Sub-Lieutenant, now aboard H.M.S. *Invincible (Camera Press/Phil Rudge)*

H.M.S. *Invincible:* weighing 16,000 tons and armed with Sea Dart anti-aircraft missiles, Sea Harriers and Sea King helicopters, she is the largest warship built for the Royal Navy since the 1950s *(Camera Press)*

The 45,000-ton luxury liner *Canberra* awaiting its refit at Southampton *(Press Association)*

Beer for the British troops *(Press Association)*

4th April 1982: Defence Secretary John Nott, right, inspects H.M.S. *Hermes* in the company of her Captain, Linley Middleton *(Press Association)*

Portsmouth, 5th April 1982: H.M.S. *Hermes,* the Task Force's flagship, sails for the South Atlantic *(Press Association)*

Men of A Company, 40 Royal Marine Commando, keeping fit on the flight deck of H.M.S. *Hermes* *(Press Association)*

The Task Force at sea
– somewhere in the
South Atlantic *(Press
Association)*

Marines from 40
Commando crouch
on the flight deck of
H.M.S. *Hermes*
during a training
session with a Sea
King helicopter *(Press
Association)*

Above: A Sea Harrier *(Daily Telegraph)*

Opposite: H.M.S. *Hermes* at dawn: Marines line up for a weapons check in brightly-lit hangar. In the background are tightly-packed Sea Harriers and Sea King helicopters *(Press Association)*

Below: A Nimrod maritime reconnaissance aircraft, right, being refuelled in-flight by an R.A.F. Victor tanker *(Press Association)*

The United Nations Secretary-General Javier Perez de Cuellar, left, with Argentine Ambassador Eduardo A. Roca in New York on 5th May 1982 *(Associated Press)*

The Argentine cruiser *General Belgrano* sinks on 2nd May 1982 after being hit by torpedoes from the British submarine *Conqueror (Associated Press)*

H.M.S. *Sheffield* which was hit by an Argentine missile on
4th May 1982, caught fire and sank subsequently *(Press
Association)*

H.M.S. *Norfolk* firing an Exocet missile similar to the one
that hit H.M.S. *Sheffield.* This photograph was taken in
1974 *(Press Association)*

The Argentine spy-ship *Narwal* captured by the British on 9th May 1982. It sank in heavy waters on 10th May 1982 *(Associated Press)*

A magazine in Buenos Aires depicts Prime Minister Margaret Thatcher as a pirate *(Associated Press)*

made for America's own purposes, the results were made available to Britain.

The Blackbirds, successors to the U2, are extraordinary aircraft. They fly at three times the speed of sound, so fast that the friction with the air raises the temperature of their skin to 1,000 degrees fahrenheit. Because of this they have to be painted a deep indigo, the most efficient colour for dissipating heat, and which has the added advantage of absorbing radar beams, making the Blackbirds virtually impossible to detect. Flying at 80,000 feet, they can make a detailed photographic survey of 100,000 square miles in an hour. Little escapes their cameras, and what does is collected by the twelve-ton Big Bird satellites. The Americans have two of these photographic satellites stationed in elliptical orbits over the Northern and Southern hemispheres. They are able to photograph objects as small as twelve inches in diameter. The southern Big Bird sent back detailed pictures of the Falklands which enabled photographic interpreters to count the number of Argentine troops and give precise details of their dispositions and weapons. This information, passed to the British, has been invaluable in planning the recapture of the islands.

But the Big Bird is slowed up, like the Russian photographic satellites, by having to parachute its film. Big Bird does it over the Pacific where its capsule is caught in mid-air by C130 Hercules transports equipped with "fishing nets". So the Americans have developed a newer system, the KH11, which is also in orbit over the South Atlantic, and this records its photographic information in digital form which it can beam to ground stations, positioned around the world, where its information is converted back into photographic form. It is likely that one of those stations has been established on Ascension Island, the forward base for the recapture of the Falklands.

The Americans have also provided Britain with a secure channel of communication by satellite for the nuclear submarines which enforced the blockade of the islands. The position of these submarines was the most important single

piece of intelligence which the Argentines needed to acquire.
The use of the American communication system has made it
that much harder for them.

In addition, British and American electronic eavesdrop-
pers combined to listen in to Argentine radio traffic, and, as
Mr Ted Rowlands, a former minister at the Foreign Office,
somewhat indiscreetly told the House of Commons, Argentina's codes are "an open book". Monitoring of Argentine
radio traffic is another of the "Elint" tasks undertaken at
Ascension Island. It is unlikely that the Argentine cryptog-
raphers could solve the British codes and one Pentagon
spokesman commented about the inequality of intelligence
gathering and interpretation: "It almost makes it an unfair
fight."

Be that as it may, the Argentines made strenuous and
brave efforts to gather information about the task force. A
merchant ship, the *Rio de la Plata*, shadowed the fleet when it
first sailed into the South Atlantic and persisted until it was
warned off by a British frigate. A Boeing 707 also shadowed
the fleet until it was chased away by Harriers. But once the
Sheffield had been destroyed, its position possibly plotted by
the Boeing, the British extended the exclusion zone to twelve
miles off the Argentine coast and treated ruthlessly anything
found in the zone. That is why the fishing vessel *Narwal* was
attacked. She was not armed but she was a spy ship with an
Argentine Navy Lieutenant Commander on board, sending
back information about the fleet's movements and after the
loss of the *Sheffield* that could not be allowed. The *Narwal's*
presence in dangerous waters is a further point in the argument about Soviet assistance to the Argentines. It is highly
unlikely that she would have been sent on what amounted to
a suicide mission if the Russians had been providing a flow of
high-grade information to Buenos Aires.

It is not necessary, of course, for intelligence to be high
grade or electronic to be useful. The British authorities
debriefing Falkland Islanders who had fled or been expelled
from the islands, were able to piece together a picture of
conditions on the islands, along with information on the

numbers, positions and morale of the occupying troops. Valuable information came from two RAF chief technicians, Keith Stuart and Noel Robson, who were on detachment at Stanley airfield but were allowed to leave by the Argentines. They came home with intelligence of what was happening at the airfield, providing especially useful confirmation that the runway had not been lengthened to take the Argentine Air Force's Mirage fighter bombers.

In addition, the task force commander was provided with a flow of information from men of the Special Boat Service and the Special Air Service who prowled the islands, seeking out landing beaches and acquiring detailed knowledge of the Argentine defences.

American reports say that these teams were given brand-new American mobile radios which link into the radio satellite system, giving them instant communication, not only with the task force but also with London, thus providing British military and political leaders with immediate news of the developing situation.

All this is grist to the intelligence mill. And there is no doubt the British obtained better information than the Argentines. But intelligence is not an end in itself. It is how it is used that matters. And that did not become apparent until later.

13

REACTIONS TO THE CRISIS
AT WESTMINSTER

In the British system of parliamentary democracy it is the duty and not simply the right of those political parties not in the government to provide loyal opposition to that government. It is a task which becomes a great deal more difficult when the guns begin to speak, and when it is clear from all expressions of public opinion that the population in general is ready to support warlike action in a national cause.

From the start of the Falklands affair, therefore, both the Labour Party and the alliance of Social Democrats and Liberals found themselves in an awkward position. The sudden crisis had taken their leaders by surprise as much as it had Mrs Thatcher and her government. The first response of Opposition leaders was to back the government's decision to mobilise the fleet in support of diplomatic action.

Mr Michael Foot, Leader of the Opposition, was well aware how sensitive the Labour Party was to actions which might lead to armed conflict. However he took a bold stand and demanded deeds not words. In this he was firmly backed by Mr Denis Healey, an old hand from the Defence Ministry and a former minister well versed in handling foreign affairs. Mr Peter Shore, the Shadow Chancellor, also advocated firm support for strong measures. That was all very well at the time when the task force sailed and the prospect of action in the South Atlantic was still weeks away, but as the reality of fighting on sea and land loomed nearer, the Labour Party leaders needed to keep looking over their shoulders. For on the parliamentary benches behind them, and in the rank-

and-file membership of the party, there were many others more apprehensive and doubting than they were.

The most numerous group in the Opposition were those loyalists ready to support the government in its determination to brandish military force. Fortunately the "enemy" was Argentina, a country which might easily be branded as Fascist, with a record unsavoury enough to convince socialist supporters that for once they were morally justified in supporting military threats. However, within the Labour Party, there has traditionally been a sizeable minority of pacifists opposed to the use of force anywhere. Mr Frank Allaun is the most vociferous member of this group, but during the Falklands crisis his voice was not alone. Mr Tam Dalyell issued several warnings of terrible naval disasters should the fleet steam into action, arguing, quite reasonably, that it had insufficient air cover against the powerful Argentine Air Force.

From the very beginning, though, the most outspoken critic of the whole enterprise, and the most effective because he is such a persuasive and seemingly logical speaker, was Mr Anthony Benn, the perpetual voice of opposition within the Opposition. Mr Benn's misgivings were greeted with howls of derision from the Tories and with expressions of deep dislike and distrust from members of his own party. Nevertheless, he spoke consistently. In his view the task force should never have sailed; when it did sail it should have been ordered to return to Portsmouth. The whole dispute over the present and the future of the Falkland Islands should have been placed at once in the hands of the United Nations, which he believed capable of resolving the whole affair. In such arguments he received strong, though less coherent, support from Dame Judith Hart, Chairman of the Labour Party.

However Mr Benn's rank-and-file supporters were disparate and extreme. This became evident when he and Dame Judith led a peace rally which brought out some 1,200 people in Hyde Park. Marching behind banners proclaiming "I am ashamed to be British", was a large contingent from the

Socialist Workers Party, campaigners for nuclear disarma-
ment, Iranian students, Methodists and Quakers. It seemed
highly unlikely that religious peace-makers would have
wanted to support cries of "Victory to the Argentines against
the British fleet", which drew many an indignant protest.
Nor can Mr Benn himself have supported the logic of
Professor Michael Prentz, Vice Chairman of CND, who
speculated that nuclear weapons might be used as a last
resort if the life of Prince Andrew, serving aboard HMS
Invincible, was threatened by an Argentine attack.

At the rally Mr Benn's comments extended to the coverage
of the crisis in the press and on the television. "The gutter
press have called us traitors," he declared, "but I believe we
represent a majority of people who don't want to see any
killing." Although he was entirely correct in believing that no
feeling of blood lust was discernible in Britain, nevertheless
the opinion polls, which indicated widespread support for
Mrs Thatcher's policies, demonstrated that he was wrong in
believing that a majority was behind him. It was not, as he
claimed, "Mrs Thatcher's War", but a well-supported campaign in a national cause.

Nonetheless, it has to be recognised that the task of
Bennites ready to go all the way in opposing government
policy was an easier one than that of the Foot–Healey
leadership. For, having bravely committed themselves to
approving government action, they then had to qualify that
support as the situation became more warlike. They had to
keep the party together without giving an impression of
disloyalty. For this reason Mr Healey concentrated upon
criticising step by step, probing for signs of incompetence,
and blaming for failure. It was not at all an easy role to play,
especially when the outcome was far from foreseeable.

As the Haig mission drew to a close and it became clear
that the American intervention had not succeeded, Mr
Healey made his first constructive suggestion. The time had
come, he said, to call upon the United Nations. "The government should immediately approach Mr Javier Perez de
Cuellar, Secretary General of the United Nations, quoting

the Security Council Resolution, to see if he will use his good offices to advance the negotiations. I believe that if he would appoint an administrator of the islands . . . this might break the deadlock and create a situation in which the Argentine troops would leave the islands. Then negotiations could proceed between Britain and Argentina.''

When in fact the UN Secretary General was called in after the collapse of the short-lived Peruvian attempt at mediation, Mr Healey was able to claim with reason that he had been the first to suggest this move. The very mention of the UN, which, despite its many shortcomings, still attracts great enthusiasm in the Labour Party, was enough to get strong backing from its MPs who were becoming increasingly worried as the task force sailed south.

The re-taking of South Georgia, and the fact that it was accomplished without losses, brought a feeling of relief among the politicians. Despite the increasingly warlike talk from Mrs Thatcher and her Cabinet, those with less stomach for a fight were beginning to think that all might yet be well. By the end of April some of the heat was going out of parliamentary debates and talk of war seemed less frightening because it had become routine. Mr Michael Foot took up the United Nations idea, and for the Opposition at least the magic initials UN seemed to offer a way out of all the difficulties. Mrs Thatcher was reasonably reproached for her lack of enthusiasm for the Secretary General. However, she struck back by quoting such an impeccable neutral as the Swedish Foreign Minister on the difficulties the UN had in enforcing its policies.

Although mutterings were growing louder in the Labour ranks, the political centre – that is to say, the SDP/Liberal Alliance – was being held firm by the leader who had been shown to greatest advantage since the crisis began, Dr David Owen. As a former Foreign Secretary, then in the Labour Party, and as a former Navy minister who moreover represented Plymouth in the House, he had staunchly backed the Tory policy of ''prepare for war but be ready for negotiation''. His firm and sensible remarks from the very begin-

ning had established him as the most effective spokesman of
the new party. He had the great advantage of having displayed a firmness of purpose when, as Foreign Secretary in 1977,
he had forestalled a previous Argentine attempt to take the
Falkland Islands.

In the debate on 29 April he summed up again; "The
government must remain free to take action . . . they alone
can make that decision. They have at least the right to ask
that, whatever doubts we may have, we will give them the
benefit of the doubt . . ." He went on to say that if it became
necessary for our servicemen to take action, they should not
be made to feel that their action was the subject of a bitter
parliamentary debate about rights and wrongs. That had
happened during the Suez campaign in 1956 when the
British invaded Egypt, and it should not happen now. Dr
Owen's statesmanlike interventions increased his standing in the SDP/Liberal alliance and there is no doubt that his
cool-headed handling of the affair has improved his chances
of leading the SDP. Mr David Steel, the Liberal leader, was a
great deal less decisive, though sensible, and among the other
alliance bosses, Mrs Williams, full of doubts and indecision,
sensibly kept quiet. So too, did Mr Roy Jenkins, the SDP
man with the best claim to experience in statesmanship.
Weeks of crisis went by before he rose to speak on the subject
in the House, and then, as Frank Johnson, the witty parliamentary commentator of *The Times* put it, "he rolled a jowl
at the Falklands," declaring: "Will the right honourable
Lady, in view of the strong all-party support which the
government has rightly received during the past two and a
half weeks, bear in mind that she will be expected to take
future, I hope and believe, unrushed decisions . . ."

By the end of April the military crunch was beginning.
Vulcan bombers flew from Ascension Island on 30 April and
a determined attack was made by it and by Royal Navy
Harriers upon the airfield at Stanley. Then, in the first week
of May, military operations firmly impinged upon Parliament at Westminster. First there was the sinking of the
Argentine cruiser, the *General Belgrano*, and hardly had the

Opposition begun probing the naval necessity of this action, demanding to know the exact position of the cruiser when she was hit, before the graver news broke of the loss of the British destroyer HMS *Sheffield*.

The sinking of the *Belgrano* dramatically posed the question of whether the British government was using too much naval muscle. Already the Opposition was worrying about the "disproportionate" use of strength. It had not granted Mrs Thatcher a "blank cheque" in the use of the task force. Was it strictly necessary to go ostentatiously sinking cruisers in order to demonstrate the soundness of a fleet-in-being theory, was the question being asked. Would not such action lose Britain the support of her friends?

Government ministers answered the former question with the argument that the first duty of the fleet was to protect itself, and the lives of the men aboard it, by shooting first. In the House of Commons Mrs Thatcher defended herself in more emotional terms: "The worry I live with hourly is that the Argentine forces might attack by sea and air and get through to our forces and sink some of our ships." It was not long before that nagging fear was justified, when the Exocet missile from the Argentines did in fact strike home, causing the loss of HMS *Sheffield*.

From the beginning the political parties had all been declaring that as few people as possible must lose their lives in whatever operations took place. The loss of the *Sheffield*, and the loss of one Harrier in action, and two by accident, brought it home to Westminster that it was not just Argentine blood which was being lamented. British lives too were being lost. For many people, and not only those who supported the Opposition, this was a demonstration that things were getting out of hand. More MPs were asking how many lives it was worth losing in order to go to the rescue of only 1,800 Falkland Islanders. It was as though the Clausewitz maxim, "war is an extension of diplomacy", was being transformed into the theory that war is an extension of accountancy. Politicians were establishing a gruesome balance sheet, measuring the value of sovereignty and 1,800 liberated Britons against so many litres of blood spilled.

The sinking of the ships was a warning signal for politicians of all parties to remind themselves of the danger of the enterprise undertaken. Reaction to the events cut across the normal party lines, for there were many in the Conservative ranks who sympathised with Mr Healey when he reiterated that emphasis should be on the "proportionate" use of force and on negotiations as well.

Mr Pym, the new Foreign Secretary, favoured greater effort towards a diplomatic solution, and after the naval actions the government as a whole was more willing to go to the UN Secretary General for help in negotiations. Bipartisanship survived, especially in the political persons of Mr Pym and Mr Healey, as Britain greatly modified her negotiating position.

By this time the big issues raised by the Falklands conflict were regularly being discussed by a restricted Cabinet group, which came to be known as the "War Cabinet". Presided over by Mrs Thatcher, it consisted of Mr Pym, Foreign Secretary, Mr Nott, the Defence Secretary, Mr William Whitelaw, the Home Secretary, and Mr Cecil Parkinson. In addition Admiral Sir Terence Lewin, Chief of Defence Staff, was called in frequently to add his military advice, and occasionally Sir Michael Havers, the Attorney General, was present. Mr Whitelaw was no doubt asked to attend because he is an experienced minister with deep political knowledge, well known for adding a word of caution. But the presence of Mr Cecil Parkinson, a minister with departmental responsibilities as Chancellor of the Duchy of Lancaster, led to criticism that he was there in his role as Chairman of the Conservative Party, even though it appeared that the War Cabinet never considered the impact of the South Atlantic crisis on party affairs. Some commentators suspected that Mr Parkinson, a loyal friend of the Prime Minister, was selected to make sure that she always had a majority within her restricted Cabinet, should Mr Pym favour a milder course of action with support from Mr Whitelaw. In fact, there were no signs of any real split of opinion.

The same could not be said of the Conservative Party itself, either in the House of Commons, or outside. From the start there had been dissenting voices. Sir Anthony Meyer, a man of impeccable Tory credentials and a former diplomat, made a reasoned declaration that he could not go along with the idea of the fleet taking offensive action in the South Atlantic. He was not alone in this view. Another former Foreign Office man, Mr Ray Whitney, also opposed the government line. As Peregrine Worsthorne, the *Sunday Telegraph*'s columnist, had commented, at the beginning of the crisis it was the common man who demanded action while the élite and in particular Tory diplomats belonged to the "wiser counsels" school of thought.

While the Tory peace-mongers were emerging – especially after the sinkings – another group began to criticise Mrs Thatcher for not being warlike enough. Its argument ran as follows; now that the fleet is in danger from the Argentine Air Force, let us send the Vulcans and bomb Argentina's mainland airfields. If that is not possible, let us base Phantoms on the airfields of friendly Chile and let them do the job. Other helpful suggestions were that the Special Air Service regiment, the SAS, might be sent to the Argentine mainland to sabotage aircraft, dumps and airfields. Among the most outspoken advocates of such dramatic action were Mr Alan Clark, Tory MP for Plymouth, Sir Bernard Braine and Mr Winston Churchill. Others in the party cast a longing eye upon such possibilities but considered that Mrs Thatcher's brand of strength was ultimately more sensible.

From his own highly original position of independence as a high but lapsed Tory, Mr Enoch Powell urged strong action and offered his support to Mrs Thatcher. He was rightly conscious of the change which had come about in British feelings since the invasion. It was a long time since he had given support to a Conservative Prime Minister, but that support was welcome. He wrote in *The Times*, "Britain has not merely asserted in theory or conditional intent its national right to recover its own territory by force. Blood has been shed. An earnest of Britain's determination to restore and to hold its own has been given in terms which are unmistakable and irreversible." In less apocalyptic terms, a number of former Prime Ministers emerged to assure the government of their encouragement, notably Mr James Callaghan, Sir Harold Wilson, Lord Hume and, up to a point, Mr Heath.

As the denouement approached, a national concensus still prevailed, finding its expression in the House of Commons through the varying voices of Mr Pym, Mr Healey, Mr Heath and Mr Foot. However it was always apparent that each of the political parties had its own war party and its own peace party. If Mr Powell represented the right of the line in the war party, Mr Benn stood on the left of the line in the peace party. But in the middle was the government, and there seemed little doubt that Mrs Thatcher firmly represented the British people in the crisis, and that her handling of that crisis had greatly impressed them. When the negotiations conducted by the UN Secretary General were showing every sign of imminent collapse, the political pressures on the government were at their height. Yet at this time the BBC's Panorama TV programme broadcast the results of a public opinion poll conducted by MORI. Ninety per cent of those questioned said they wanted the immediate withdrawal of all Argentine forces. No less than fifty-nine per cent said they wanted an invasion of the islands if negotiations broke down, while only nineteen per cent said they would settle for an extended blockade.

This firmness of purpose translated itself into support for the government and the poll indicated that forty-eight per cent would vote Conservative if an election were held in mid May. This represented a ten per cent increase since a similar poll by the same organisation ten days earlier. Thirty-three per cent said they would vote for the Labour Party.

The hard wing of the Tory party, which had begun to accuse Mrs Thatcher of readiness to sell out to the Argentines, must have been reassured by such figures. In any case the Prime Minister made her position absolutely clear in a broadcast on Monday, 17 May. Britain, she said, was having "one more go" at the United Nations "to see if we can persuade them [the Argentines] to pull back." She went on, "My guess is that we shall know this week whether we're going to get a peaceful settlement or not." But, if the Argentine junta refused to withdraw its forces from the occupied islands, Mrs Thatcher declared, "Then I'm afraid we will have to use force to get them out."

Members of Parliament could hardly complain that they were not being kept informed by the government. The sixth parliamentary debate on the conflict was arranged for 20 May and before that the Prime Minister gave an up-to-date confidential briefing on what is called "Privy Council" terms, to Dr Owen of the SDP and Mr David Steel, the Liberal leader. Mr Foot, for the Labour Party, had earlier refused to attend such meetings on the grounds that they might inhibit his questioning in Parliament. However he did ask the Prime Minister to give time for the House of Commons to debate the merits of peace proposals before any further major military escalation. Mrs Thatcher refused, saying bluntly that no military action could be held up in that way as, "to do so would be to give notice to the dictator who is our enemy." In any case, under the British constitution, foreign policy and war are the prerogatives of the government, though of course their decisions may be challenged later in the House of Commons.

As the talking came to an end at the United Nations and the signs multiplied that the task force would soon strike back in the Falklands, the critics in the Tory Party, who had feared what they called a "sell-out", were stilled. This served only to excite further the suspicions of Labour Party left-wingers and pacifists who had all along been critical of the harder line leadership of Mr Foot and Mr Healey.

In the sixth parliamentary debate of the crisis, and the last before action was joined, Anthony Benn and Dame Judith Hart divided the House of Commons in a vote. Although the bulk of the Labour Party abstained, the Bennite rump mustered thirty-three votes disapproving of government action. It was the first time that votes had been cast against the strong policy of Mrs Thatcher and it also amounted to a declaration of civil war in the Labour Party. But if some politicians on the left thus showed signs of wavering, public opinion remained strongly in favour of a British assault upon the islands to liberate them from the invader.

As the landings began on Friday, 21 May, a poll taken for London Weekend Television indicated that seventy-six per cent favoured the assault, and fifty-three per cent considered that a successful operation was worth heavy casualties.

14

THE FALKLAND ISLANDERS

The day that President Galtieri flew into the airfield at Stanley to celebrate his triumph and to install General Mario Benjamin Menendez as Military Governor of the occupied islands, it was blowing a gale. To the satisfaction of Falkland Islanders who watched the ceremony, the force of the wind broke the flagstaff on Secretariat Green and the blue and white Argentine flag hit the ground during the swearing-in ceremony.

This incident was reported in a letter to a relation in Britain from a Falkland Islander who added, "This was considered a very bad omen by the Argentines." The fact that such a letter could have been written at all shows something of the spirit of the British people of the islands at a time when their worst fears had just been realised. For years the population of 1,800 souls had been well aware that there was little to prevent Argentine forces, based only 400 miles away, from seizing their islands. Now it had come to pass. The cheerful British diplomat Mr Rex Hunt had flown off into forced exile. The defending Royal Marines had been defeated and now a hard-line Argentine general was in control of the islands, with an army at least four times the size of the local population to enforce his laws.

Yet the people who stayed behind were still able to write cheerful letters to their relations back home. One of them reported on the group of Anglo-Argentines resident on the mainland who had been flown to Stanley with the aim of persuading the islanders that life under junta rule was not too bad. "Well, their visit was only for a few hours, they spent a lot of it buying up British goods and Falkland wool, etc, at West Store," reported the correspondent, scarcely disguising the irony.

There can be no doubt that the invasion alarmed the islanders and produced an initial mood of deep depression. The way of life which they enjoyed had suddenly been shot away from under them. General Menendez, a fifty-two-year-old military man who speaks little English, began decreeing the kind of irksome military rules so much favoured by occupying armies. There were curfews and a proclamation was issued to the effect that penalties ranging from seven to 180 days' imprisonment might be awarded to anyone who failed to respect the rules, insulted Argentina or aggravated the soldiers. The most obvious sign that the islands were under new and foreign management was that motorists were ordered to drive on the right-hand side of the road, and it was made clear that the Britons would be expected to learn Spanish. Spreading false information was also made an offence. All these measures bore the stamp of an oppressor's jackboot.

Even more sinister indications soon appeared. The military took over the office and home of Colonel Ron Lamb, head of the local police, replacing him by Major Patricio Dowling, an Argentine Army intelligence officer. Shortly after this Major Dowling, accompanied by twelve armed soldiers, helicoptered to the farm of Mr William Luxton whose family have sheep-farmed on the Falklands for over a century. They searched the farm and ordered Mr Luxton into the helicopter. He was told that the authorities had compiled a dossier on him because of a speech he had made eight years ago. The Major added: "Oh yes, we have files on many people, nearly 500." Mr Luxton was deported, on the grounds that he was a subversive influence. The islanders found this Anglo-Argentine officer very alarming. "We called him the Gauleiter," said Colonel Lamb, "party because of his Alsatian dogs, but mostly because of his cold, creepy manner."

Falkland Islanders are, by nature, independent and sturdy people, well-informed about current affairs, despite the lack

of television, by their regular listening to the BBC overseas
news programmes. What distressed them particularly during this time was the feeling of isolation. The British government had never shown much sympathy with their desire to
remain British and independent. In the first week of occupation it seemed to them unlikely that their compatriots would
even consider going to war just to rescue 1,800 people, the
population of a small British village. Then, as it became
clearer that there was a new mood back home in Britain, and
that a battle fleet was actually sailing south to the rescue,
thoughtful people on the Falklands began wondering what
would happen to them if a battle were to break out on their
forlorn islands.

The easiest escape route was provided by the fact that
LADE, the airline run by the Argentine Air Force initially
continued its weekly flight from Stanley to Comodoro Rivadavia. Of the native born Falkland Islanders, only twenty-
one took this way out and made their way to Britain. The
majority were reluctant to abandon their homes, their pos-
sessions and the islands where they had lived their lives.
Between eighty and a hundred other Britons who were
temporarily resident there, with their families, as function-
aries of the British government, also left.

Of the remaining population over half the 1,000 people
who lived in Stanley, the only real town, thought it prudent
to stay with friends and relations in the small settlements and
sheep farms scattered through the islands. Mrs Lorraine
McGill was with her two children on a visit to Stanley when
the Argentines invaded. Bravely she made her way back to
Carcass Island, off West Falkland, where she, her husband
Rob and their two children are the only residents. Her
journey was typical of many islanders as they made their way
to safety in the country, passing many Argentine road blocks.

Many older people firmly refused to leave their homes in
Stanley. So when the fighting started there were nearly 300
British people still in the town. They were surrounded by the
strongest concentrations of the Argentine occupying force,
and therefore in the greatest danger. It was noticeable that

those who owned their own homes, as opposed to those who lived in houses belonging to the Falkland Islands Company (the consortium which virtually bought the islands in 1851), were the most reluctant to leave Stanley.

Among those who stayed behind in the islands, morale improved greatly with the news that the Royal Marines storming party had recaptured South Georgia in such a swift operation and with so few casualties. There was renewed hope that the same kind of operation might be repeated in the Falklands themselves. This optimism was reinforced by what the islanders had seen of the Argentine Army at first hand. They discovered that the invading battalions were largely composed of young conscripts, who were cold, wet and sometimes hungry. They did not look in any way as formidable as the detachments of Royal Marines whom the islanders knew as friends in the pubs of Stanley.

It should come as no surprise that with the Falkland Islanders, as with any other group of British citizens, opinion was far from unanimous. When he flew out to England, Mr Edmund Carlisle, part owner of a sheep farm, implored his compatriots, "For God's sake do not invade." He said he wanted to tell Mrs Thatcher it would be madness to retake the islands by force and that the islanders did not want military action. He believed they could prosper under Argentine rule. "Attitudes have changed remarkably in the week since invasion," he said. He was speaking before the South Georgia operation had taken place. After that, and until the first air raids on Stanley airfield cut the mail service, letters were still coming out which clearly showed that the islanders had lost none of their courage. It seems clear that the first British Harrier shot down must have crashed within 150 yards of the settlement at Goose Green, where 114 people were living surrounded by a battalion of Argentine troops. Yet even after these first raids, a trickle of courageous telegrams still came out of Stanley. "Still well, and kicking," was the text of one of them. A delayed letter which eventually arrived in England told of incidents in the supermarket in Stanley. When Argentine customers offered payment in

pesos, the woman at the cash desk handled them gingerly
and then rather pointedly washed her hands with disinfec-
tant. Such stories of minor displays of resistance to alien rule
helped to cheer the islanders.

John Cheek, an elected member of the Falklands Legisla-
tive Council was in London when the invasion started. From
such indications and from his knowledge of fellow citizens on
the islands, he drew the conclusion that the people were
standing up well to the long period of waiting which followed
South Georgia's liberation. They would have seen the effects
of British air raids at first hand, for the main airport is very
close to Stanley. They would certainly have heard of the
naval actions in news bulletins and would know about
commando raids on shore. Mr Cheek, whose family has lived
for five generations on the islands, believes that Falkland
people would have welcomed the military action to release
them from Argentine control. The swift, armed action would
have been considered preferable to a long, drawn-out blockade.

After the commando raid on Pebble Island, General
Menendez, the Military Governor, claimed on Argentine TV
that Falkland Islanders were perhaps in touch with the
British fleet by radio, even though the authorities had early
on confiscated most transmitters. It was likely enough that
the local people would have given any help needed to the
British forces. But the Royal Marines had already put ashore
highly trained men of the Special Boat Service, who were
much better equipped with electronics and tactical knowledge to send intelligence to the ships. The islanders knew
that should the Argentines discover that they were helping
the SBS, there would be reprisals, and this is a further
indication of their passive resistance.

During the crisis a great deal was written about the normal
conditions of the Falklands. One misconception that arose
was of the continuously appalling weather. Mr Cheek, who
was a meteorologist before joining Cable and Wireless, had
a different story to tell. Visibility is usually good – about
thirty-five miles – and only a couple of times a year was it

impossible for the weekly Fokker airliner to get in from
Comodoro Rivadavia. There is a good deal of wind but the
average rainfall in Stanley, which usually comes in drizzle
rather than in rain storms, is a modest twenty-three inches a
year.

The other misconception was about the Britons of the
Falkland Islands, usually described by television commentators and newspapermen as "more British than the British",
and rather out of date in their ways and thoughts. The truth
of the matter is that their lifestyle, though simple, is very
similar to that of English, Welsh and Scottish people living in
small country places.

The islands depend on the wool trade controlled by the
Falkland Islands Company which is now a subsidiary of the
British firm, Coalite. The company is responsible for a
million and a quarter acres with about 300,000 sheep on its
farms. Some 700 Falklanders are involved with the company.
They consider that their way of life compares favourably
with that of people in Buenos Aires and, come to that, in
London. When members of the Anglo-Argentine community
on the mainland suggested that a truce might be called so
that a neutral ship could go to Stanley to take off the 300
children remaining in the Falklands, it was firmly rejected.
The islanders said they had no wish to see their children
taken to Argentina, and preferred that they should take their
chances at home.

However, the detentions continued. In mid-May Mr John
Cheek received a worrying letter from his father in Stanley,
reporting that his brother Gerald and a number of prominent
men in the island had been taken from their homes by
Argentine troops. Apart from Gerald Cheek, the local civil
aviation director, they had arrested Dr Daniel Haines, the
medical officer, and a local radio officer. It was thought that
they had been moved with several others to a detention
centre at Fox Bay. The letter, which had been sent at the end
of April and before the air raids, was post stamped "Puerto
Argentina". It contained references to "visitors" being
everywhere in the island. News of the arrests fortified fears

about what might happen if the Argentines remained in control for long, and reminded islanders of the sinister blacklist of dossiers mentioned by Major Patricio Dowling.

The Falklands conflict also had its effect upon other British people living away from the United Kingdom. In Argentina itself there are at least 17,000 British passport-holders who were advised to leave the country early in the affair, if only until passions cooled. Although the Argentine authorities announced that they would guarantee the safety of such expatriates, there were fears of local reaction when the task force went into action.

Apart from the passport-holders, it was estimated that there were at least 30,000, and possibly up to 100,000, members of the Anglo-Argentine community who claimed British descent. One of them commented on his sadness about the Falklands crisis. "The islands aside, there is a great deal of mutual admiration between Britons and Argentines here," he said. That was no doubt true, but a step taken by members of the Association of British and British-descended Farmers in Argentina, caused ill-feeling in London. Their telegram to Mrs Thatcher showed how badly they had judged the mood in Britain. It warned that the retaking of the islands would "create damage out of all proportion to the value of the islands". Nor did the Anglican Bishop in Buenos Aires, Dr Richard Cutts, win much favour with the Prime Minister when he sent her a telegram asking her to negotiate a settlement so that Falkland Islanders could work in peace under Argentine rule as contentedly as those Britons living in Argentina. He offered to fly to Stanley with a deputation to explain what he called the "realities of living under Argentine rule". He was promptly telephoned from the Archbishop of Canterbury's office, to be told that the Falklands were removed from his diocesan control, and that he was forbidden to leave Argentina.

The expatriates in Argentina gave the impression that they were perfectly happy to live under the Argentine government, though they feared the repercussions of the conflict. For the most part they prospered there, but for them to urge the Falkland Islanders to accept Argentine rule after being invaded by Argentine troops, whether it brought them prosperity or not, seemed in Stanley and in London to be totally unsuitable.

15

THE MILITARY BUILD-UP AND THE RECAPTURE OF SOUTH GEORGIA

It was only during this later stage in the crisis that the full scale of the British preparations, the efficiency with which they were organised and the whole-heartedness with which they were carried out began to be appreciated.

The roll-call of Britain's merchant fleet was searched and ship after ship chartered or requisitioned until some hundred vessels were assembled into a motley but highly effective 8,000-mile-long shuttle of men and supplies. The liners *Canberra* and the *Queen Elizabeth II*, Britain's greatest ship; the roll-on roll-off ferry *Elk* whose captain, John Morton, cajoled the Navy into cutting away the deck structure to make an operations pad for three helicopters and to mount two ancient Bofors anti-aircraft guns in the bows; the Hull trawlers *Northella*, *Farnella*, *Junella* and *Cordella* pressed into service as minesweepers; and the fruit ship *Geestport* was chartered to supply frozen food to the ships of the task force; they and scores of others took their place in the Falklands supply shuttle.

The dockyards worked round the clock to fit them out. The *Uganda*, normally used for schoolchildren's educational cruises, was turned into a hospital ship complete with casualty helicopter pad, in just two days in Gibraltar by workers who face redundancy when the shipyard is closed next year. In British dockyards, men abandoned the traditional demarcation of jobs and worked day and night to get the ships ready for war.

It was not only in the dockyards that work went on round the clock. The workforce of Berghaus, a small company

specialising in outdoor clothing and camping equipment in
County Durham spent a weekend working flat out to complete a government order for "Igloo" suits and rucksacks
destined for the Falklands. And when it came to load the
vessels with arms and ammunition and stores of war, it
hardly seemed possible that so much of so many different
kinds of equipment could be stored in peacetime and dispatched to the quaysides at the right time and in the right
order for loading.

But some stores are not kept in large quantities; the
Tigerfish computerised torpedoes, and the Sea Cat and Sea
Dart anti-aircraft missiles, are all too expensive to maintain
in great numbers. When it became obvious that this was
going to be the world's first blooding of missiles in a naval
battle, orders were hurriedly placed and representatives of
the large companies which design the missiles, Marconi
among them, went round the country seeking out small
specialist companies to put together rush orders of components for guidance systems. Other British companies were still
filling orders for components of the French Exocet missile
with which both the Royal Navy and the Argentine Navy are
equipped – having first made sure that the French manufac-
turers, Aerospatiale, were no longer sending their deadly
weapons to Argentina.

All this activity produced a sort of mini-boom, especially
in industries which had little to look forward to. At Portsmouth, where more than 1,000 jobs are due to be lost by
1984, and the first 180 redundancy notices had already been
issued, and at Chatham, where the dockyard is due to close
by 1984 with 7,000 jobs lost, there was much satisfaction
when it was announced that the redundancies had been
postponed. By accident the conflict forced the government into doing what Mrs Thatcher said she never would do:
pump money into the economy. Some dock workers earned
twice their normal amount of pay through overtime.

Although the extra money was welcome and there was
much satisfaction among the workers at the way in which
they had proved their worth, that was not the sum of the

matter. They did it not only because they felt it was their duty but also because they wanted to demonstrate to the government that their skills and their dockyards are needed. One union official argued: "We have proved that we are needed. If this crisis had come a year later we could not have produced a fleet like this." The determination with which they went about the task of turning merchant vessels of all sorts into a powerful fleet reflected the feeling of the nation that the Argentines had gone too far and that we were not going to be bullied by a particularly unpleasant form of military dictatorship.

Naturally, not everyone was in agreement. Mr Cartwright, a Communist and Chairman of the Felixstowe branch of the National Union of Seamen, told the crews of the requisitioned commercial ferries, *Nordic Ferry* and *Baltic Ferry*, that it would be "folly" to sign on for a "dangerous adventure". Some of the men heeded his advice but their places were immediately taken by volunteers. Later, the NUS, with 2,000 members sailing for the South Atlantic, became the first big union to endorse the use of force if negotiations failed.

Meanwhile the great ships and the small ships, ships of all sizes, for all purposes, sailed on. The container ship *Atlantic Conveyor* of 15,000 tones was converted to take Harriers to reinforce the outnumbered pilots of the task force. Two thousand tons of tenting was also loaded on board her to protect the landing force against the Falklands' winter. Work began on her sister ship, the *Atlantic Causeway*, to convert her into a makeshift aircraft carrier complete with the "ski-lift" ramp which enables the Harriers to take off with a full load of weapons and fuel. At the other end of the scale, the cable ship *Iris*, only 3,873 tons, was requisitioned to act as a dispatch vessel with the fleet. It was agreed at an emergency meeting of the National Maritime Board that a Merchant Navy seaman going into the war zone should be paid a 150 per cent bonus so that a man normally earning £100 a week would be paid £250 in the danger area. Ships were requisitioned and chartered with such urgency that owners agreed to their use before working out details of payments, but by the end of the first week in May the government had paid £12,450,000 for requisitioned ships and £9,000,000 for tanker charters. In the same time P&O had received £5,400,000 for its liners *Canberra* and *Uganda* and the ferry *Elk*. It was estimated that, overall, it would cost the government at least £10 million for the use of Cunard's *Queen Elizabeth II*.

One ship was missing from the fleet, a ship which many people thought ought to have been there: the Royal Yacht *Britannia*. Critics of its expense have always been placated with the assurance that she had been designed to be converted quickly into a hospital ship in time of war. Now it was said that she could not serve this purpose because she had never undergone conversion to burn diesel instead of heavy furnace fuel. Predictably, Mr Bob Cryer, Labour MP for Keighley, attacked the decision not to send her: "It is obvious that the claim that *Britannia* could be used as a hospital ship was nothing more than a subterfuge to get the expenditure through Parliament." But even Mr Cryer was not as chagrined as the yacht's crew who made it clear they felt that they and their ship ought to be going to the South Atlantic.

Few men wanted to be left out of this enterprise. As Captain Dennis Scott-Masson, master of the *Canberra*, explained: "I shall take the ship wherever the Commander in Chief of the Royal Navy decides to send me. I have no fear whatsoever that anything might happen to my crew or my ship . . . Enormous alterations are being made to the ship and although the hairdressing and entertainments staff all volunteered to sail with us I felt they were not necessary and reluctantly turned them down."

So the ships which were to service the longest supply line in the history of warfare sailed off to gather round Ascension Island, where RAF Hercules transports were rumbling in hour after hour, day after day, bringing in supplies and men, and where helicopters swung over the coast with loads suspended beneath them to drop on to ships. Other ships ranged alongside each other to transfer loads across decks.

Tanker ships arrived carrying not only fuel but water because the island's meagre supplies could not cope with the sudden influx of thirsty men who not only threatened the water supplies but also the island's even more meagre supply of beer. The Americans were also busy, helping to operate the satellite communications system and bringing in aviation fuel to top up the island's tanks.

Then there were the secret preparations to receive the Vulcan bombers, the obsolete nuclear-deterrent aircraft which were due to be retired from the RAF in a couple of months' time. With them arrived their former V-bomber partners, the Victors, which also had become aerial tankers. The Vulcans had been rapidly converted at their base in Waddington, Lincolnshire, to take conventional instead of nuclear bombs and were then sent to practise dropping them on a range off the north coast of Scotland.

While these more eye-catching preparations were being made, the men of the Royal Marines and the Parachute Regiment, the "Booties" and the "Paras" who were to follow the initial force of some 1,000 sailing with the task force, made their own arrangements. Tough young men, battle-hardened in Belfast's back streets and the "bandit country" around Crossmaglen, they had the advantage over their naval and RAF colleagues of having heard shots fired in anger. Some of the aircrew may have been involved in putting down the insurrection in Oman and some of the old sailors may have seen action during the "confrontation" with Indonesia; but Suez in 1956 was the last time the RAF and the Navy had been involved in major operations. Korea, in 1950, was the last time they had tangled with anything really nasty. The soldiers, on the other hand, had a decade of battle experience in Northern Ireland. (The troubles in Northern Ireland have been helpful in another way. Surgeons at the Royal Victoria Hospital in Belfast have become the world's foremost experts on gunshot wounds caused by modern high-velocity rifles, and before the hospital ship *Uganda* set sail, a dossier on their life-saving techniques was delivered to surgeons on board the ship.)

These vagaries of service life led to the somewhat curious situation where men like Colonel Tom Secombe, commander of the soldiers on board the *Canberra* and destined to become Deputy Brigade Commander of the landing force, had seen action in Cyprus, Borneo, Aden and Northern Ireland while Rear Admiral Woodward, the task force commander had seen none at all until the guns began to speak in the South Atlantic. However, the captain of HMS *Invincible*, Jeremy Black, had fought in both Korea and Borneo. But the conflict in the South Atlantic was to be a very different sort of war.

While the supply and reinforcement system was gathering strength and momentum, the men and ships at the head of the task force, sailed down to the South Atlantic, training as they went to build a cohesive force to recapture the Falklands by force should the diplomacy fail. Sea Harriers practised landing and taking-off from *Invincible* and *Hermes* and then moved on to bombing and straffing runs. Sea King and Lynx helicopters joined them at weapons practice in their gunship and rocketing roles, and clattered incessantly between the ships exchanging stores and men. They brought together the captains for long sessions at which plans for the assault on the islands were thrashed out.

The air was full of the noise of planes and helicopters and the explosion of weapons as the Marines practised with their small arms and machine-guns and rockets, firing at targets thrown over the stern. The radars circled constantly while the surface-to-air Sea Darts and Sea Cats swung on their launchers tracking Harriers acting as the enemy. The quick-firing 4.5 guns added their noise to the din, pumping out twenty shells a minute with high accuracy. And then, when the ships reached within submarine range of Argentina the Sea King ASW helicopters went to work in earnest. Armed with depth charges and anti-submarine torpedoes, they patrolled round the fleet, dropping their sonar detectors into the sea, listening and watching for the enemy whose presence was looming ahead.

There was some criticism that the task force was taking too

long to get into position but it needed all the time it could get in order to weld together its disparate collection of men, machines and ships into an efficient fighting force. There was a sort of military illogic about it all for they were sailing to fight an old-fashioned war for which they had not been trained, with sophisticated weaponry designed to be used against quite a different enemy. And the enemy they were about to face was armed, because of the financial realities of weapon design and salesmanship, with many of the same weapons which were no less potent because they had been grafted on to older ships. Both fleets had the French-built Exocet ship-killing missiles, both had British-built Sea Dart and Sea Cat anti-aircraft missile systems. Sea King helicopters were in service in both fleets and the Argentines had two Type 42 class destroyers, sister ships of three of the task force destroyers. At the front of this book, we reproduce a chart showing the comparative forces, but early in the conflict none of the balance-of-power charts showed the Tigerfish computerised torpedoes of the British nuclear submarines or the Argentine Super Etendard naval strike planes and the airborne version of the Exocet which had been mated to them. These were weapons which were going to make both sides revise their estimates of the other's destructive ability.

It took the carriers of the task force three weeks and two days to reach their zone of operations and on the way the force suffered its first casualty, a crewman on a Sea King helicopter which had engine trouble and had ditched in rough seas. It was in fact extraordinary in an operation mounted with such speed and involving so much heavy equipment and flying that accidents were so rare – although one marine lost two fingers when he caught a shark but failed to make sure it was dead before trying to remove the hook. The Sea King accident, sad as it was, served to remind everyone in the task force that they were engaged in a military enterprise and some of them were certain to die before it ended.

Another casualty – slightly wounded – was Rear Admiral Woodward who wandered into the minefield of press relations and politics. He made it clear to a reporter with the task force that he had no orders which allowed him to fire first if he met the Argentine fleet outside the exclusion zone. In fact he would have to allow them to shoot first before he could defend himself. An embarrassed Defence Ministry would have preferred Sandy Woodward to keep his worries out of print and it was forced into a promise that his "rules of engagement" would be reviewed as he sailed further south.

The embarrassment was forgotten when, on Sunday, 25 April, frigates which had sailed ahead of the main force landed Marines to recapture South Georgia Island where the crisis had started with the arrival of the Argentine scrap merchants. It was a successful operation, only a skirmish in military terms, but one which was to have deep political repercussions.

South Georgia is one of the world's mostly unlikely places to have a battle. It is dominated by a mountain range with peaks rising to 10,000 feet, and glaciers marching to the sea. Winter is an extreme experience there with temperatures never rising above freezing point and the wind, which normally blows at twenty miles an hour, gusting up to eighty miles an hour on rough days. It is a little piece of Antarctica which has found its way north. Yet it has been well-used for a century and a half, first by whalers and sealers and then by scientists engaged in long-term projects studying seals, seabirds, penguins and an improbable herd of reindeer originally imported from Scotland.

But South Georgia was the obvious choice for the task force to commence the shooting war. There was little danger of civilian casualties, the Argentines had established only a small garrison of troops and they were far beyond the range of the Argentine land-based air-cover. If the *Veinticinco de Mayo* could be tempted out to fly its Skyhawks against the assault force, so much the better because by this time the nuclear-powered submarines were on station and were waiting in ambush.

The shooting started with a curious incident on Sunday, 25 April, a "first" in a conflict which was to be full of such "blooding" of weaponry: British helicopters found and disabled an Argentine submarine with depth charges, rockets and machine-gun fire. The submarine, the *Sante Fé*, was an American Guppy class submarine, launched in 1945, and bought, reconditioned, from the United States. She was running into the sheltered anchorage of Grytviken with supplies and forty Marine reinforcements for the garrison when it was spotted on the surface by two helicopters. What happened next was described by a lieutenant commander who piloted one of the Lynx helicopters: "Visibility was not good but we could see the submarine about a mile away. The first helicopter had dropped a depth charge on to the submarine and had then returned to get more weapons. We launched an anti-submarine weapon. By this time the submarine was obviously damaged. We were not sure how badly damaged she was or whether she was able to dive. Our main aim was to remove what capacity she had and so we attacked, making passes over her with the machine-gun.

"Our purpose was to destroy her periscope and radar in the conning tower. On the third pass we realised that some bullets were in fact coming the other way.

"Two men in the conning tower were firing some form of machine-gun. I don't know how far the bullets came towards us, but they missed. We were certainly hitting her with our fire, judging from the number of ricochets. While we were looking down on the submarine a helicopter from another ship fired two missiles at the submarine. The first one hit the port side of the conning tower. By this time she was steering a fairly erratic course, leaking a fair amount of oil."

The helicopters then came under fire from machine-guns on shore and the submarine just managed to limp into the jetty where her sixty-man crew and the Marine reinforcements ran for cover.

The exact sequence of events in South Georgia remained unclear until the publication of a letter written by Leigh Currey, an eighteen-year-old radar operator on HMS *Antrim*, one of the two large destroyers with the task force. In it he told his father that two Wessex helicopters, one of them from

the 27,400 ton Royal Fleet auxiliary vessel *Tidespring*, had
crashed in a blizzard on the island three days before the 120
men of M Company, nicknamed "The Mighty Munch", of
42 Commando were landed at Grytviken. Faced with this
letter the Ministry of Defence spokesman Mr Ian McDonald
admitted that the helicopters had crashed but that
there was no announcement at the time for "operational
reasons".

"In this kind of thing," he maintained, "the less that is
said the better because of one project perhaps reflecting
another." His embarrassment was caused by the fact that the
helicopters had been landing members of the Special Boat
Service and the Special Air Service to reconnoitre for the
landing and undertake certain undercover tasks. These men,
belonging to Britain's two elite units, are acknowledged as
the best "special" soldiers in the world, with a reputation for
courage and expertise dating from the private war they
fought against the Germans in the Second World War. It was
generally assumed that they would be prowling round South
Georgia and the Falklands, landing from helicopters, canoes,
submarines or even high-altitude parachute drops, long
before an assault would be made. But nobody was going to
thank Leigh Currey for confirming the fact.

It seems, however, that South Georgia was crawling with
British soldiers for days before the landing.

Certainly one marine was landed well before the assault.
He arrived by helicopter to protect the film-makers Miss
Cindy Buxton and Miss Annie Price and they took film of
him teaching them how to use a Browning 9mm pistol. He
came, said Miss Buxton, from HMS *Endurance*. In fact
Endurance had never moved far away from South Georgia and
had linked up with the strike force to provide a communications headquarters and take on the Marines from the
cramped confines of the frigates.

A Royal Artillery officer was also well established before
M Company arrived. Unnamed for security reasons, he later
told a group of correspondents on board *Invincible* that he had
established an artillery observation post on high ground

overlooking Grytviken. From there he could see the Argentine garrison and the area where the British troops planned to land. "I could see there were people milling around the area of King Edward Point and an Argentine flag was flying. I could not see any definite enemy position; only what appeared a strange-looking twisted object which later turned out to be a helicopter which had been shot down by Royal Marines when they defended the island against the Argentines four weeks ago.

"I then commenced a bombardment of the shore but was not allowed to engage targets closer than 800 yards from the enemy position. I was very careful not to do that because at that stage we merely wished to demonstrate superior fire power and to clear the area that would be required to be used by our own troops.

"We were not actually firing at the enemy with our heavy guns. Firing continued until ground forces were established three hours later and the white flag went up.

"The surrender was in fact before the ground forces came within small arms range – the enemy never fired a shot. I think the naval gunfire must have had a very demoralising effect on the enemy, especially since the fire was brought down around them in a controlled pattern so that they obviously were able to observe that we could have hit them if we wanted to."

The next day the small garrison at Leith, along the coast, also surrendered and along with them the scrap metal merchants whose arrival on South Georgia had started the whole extraordinary affair.

It was an entirely satisfactory episode for the British. The island had been recaptured from the aggressor. The scientists had been rescued and Miss Buxton and Miss Price had taken their own film of Grytviken once again under British rule, showing the *Santa Fé* lying, holed, in shallow water and the wreckage of the Puma shot down by Lieutenant Mills and his men several weeks before, a neat piece of propaganda which seemed to be beyond the ability of the Defence Ministry's press department.

The Marines, commanded by Major Guy Sheridan, had had a taste of action, the Vickers Mark 8 4.5 guns of the frigates had proved their worth in demoralising a land-based enemy with the accuracy of their shooting. The Galtieri regime had suffered its first military setback. A springboard had been obtained for the assault on the Falklands, 800 miles west. The Grytviken anchorage would provide a haven for ships lashed by the fearsome winter storms of the South Atlantic and shipbound soldiers could be given a run ashore. There was even a possibility that the bulldozers carried by the back-up fleet could clear an airstrip to be laid with the steel "Lego" prefabricated runway known to have been loaded on one of the ships.

All this had been done with no British casualties whatsoever and with only one Argentinian wounded, a sailor from the *Santa Fé* who lost the lower part of one leg. The signal announcing this success was sent, Navy-style, to the Admiralty: "Be pleased to inform Her Majesty that the White Ensign flies alongside the Union Jack on South Georgia. God Save the Queen."

No wonder that Mrs Thatcher appeared before the television cameras outside No 10 Downing Street to tell the nation that it should "Rejoice . . . Rejoice . . ."

There was indeed cause for satisfaction. It was an efficient start to the campaign. But war is rarely an occasion for unallayed rejoicing and the success at South Georgia was marred by a curious incident in which an Argentine prisoner, Sub-Officer Primera F. Arthur, was shot dead while the *Santa Fé* was being moved from the jetty at Grytviken. He was buried with full military honours and a Court of Inquiry was set up to establish how he died. The Argentines were informed through the Red Cross but until now no further details of the incident have been released because of "legal processes and obligations". It is believed, however, that Sub-Officer Arthur was shot while attempting to sabotage the *Santa Fé* to prevent it being moved.

Then there was the extraordinary case of Captain Alfredo Astiz, commander of the garrison, who officially surrendered

to Captain David Pentreath of the frigate *Plymouth* and
Captain Nicholas Barker of the *Endurance*.

The surrender was carried out with punctilious ceremony
in the wardroom of the *Plymouth* and the instrument of
surrender, written in copperplate handwriting on notepaper
headed with the joint crests of HMS *Endurance* and HMS
Plymouth, read much as it would have done in Nelson's time:
"By this means I surrender unconditionally the base of Leith
and its surroundings in the name of the Argentine government to representatives of Her Britannic Majesty's Royal
Navy this day, the 26th of April 1982." Captain Astiz did
add: "Due to the superiority of enemy forces I am handing
myself over to British forces." The ceremony over, he and the
captain of the *Santa Fé* were entertained to dinner by the
British officers. They were treated as honourable men and in
turn they expressed their gratitude for the humanity being
shown to the prisoners.

Then questions began to be asked about Captain Astiz.
Was he a man of honour and humanity or was he a man of
the same name, notorious as one of Argentina's most cruel
torturers? The French and the Swedes were particularly
interested in him. According to French press reports he was
"Captain Death", one of the most sadistic interrogators at
the Argentine Navy Engineering School in Buenos Aires,
where several thousand left-wing prisoners were "proces-
sed" and many of them were never heard of again. Sweden
wanted to question him about the fate of seventeen-year-old
Dagmar Hagelin who, according to eye witnesses, was shot
in the back by Captain Astiz and was last seen in 1978 in
prison, lame as the result of her wounds, and chained to a
bed. The French wanted to question Astiz about the disappearance of two nuns, Sisters Alice Domon and Renée-
Leonie Duquet. Both governments made official requests to
the British to allow them to interrogate Astiz, requests which
proved embarrassing because he was classed as a "prisoner
of hostilities" under the Geneva Convention. However, when
the other prisoners from South Georgia were repatriated
through Uruguay, Captain Astiz was not with them. He was

kept behind under close guard on Ascension Island.

Then Rear Admiral Woodward ran into political trouble again. Justifiably delighted with the success of the South Georgia operation, he told correspondents that it was only the "appetiser" for "the big match" which he said should be "a walk-over". But a couple of days later in another interview he warned that the Falklands crisis "could become a long and bloody campaign".

These statements provided ammunition for Mrs Thatcher's political opponents, drew from her the remark that "the comments of the task force commander are always vivid, if various," and earned him a rebuke from his superiors.

Nevertheless he had eventually come to the correct assessment of the situation. The campaign was about to become bloody.

16

THE CONTINUED DIPLOMATIC EFFORTS TO FIND A PEACEFUL SOLUTION

After Mr Haig's return to Washington a gloomy view was being taken of the possibility of settling the crisis by shuttle diplomacy. As the commander of the British task force began tightening the blockade round the islands, there was an obvious need for a British initiative. On Thursday, 22 April, Francis Pym, the Foreign Secretary, flew to Washington by Concorde.

There seemed little chance that by seeing Mr Haig on his home ground he could put together any new ideas for persuading the Argentines towards a conference table, but at least his presence in the United States might help in the essential task of winning American support for the British position. Without such powerful backing it would be unthinkable to order the task force to go into action.

All that Mr Pym had time to do during his thirty-six hour visit was to discuss matters again with Mr Haig and put together a document examining the problem thoroughly. The Foreign Secretary commented in the language of diplomacy that he supposed this might be interpreted as a form of progress.

President Galtieri did not help matters by choosing this moment to fly to the Falkland Islands, partly to demonstrate that they were now firmly under Argentine control, and partly for the prestige and pleasure of being seen and photographed with his conquering troops upon the disputed territory. He was so moved by the occasion that tears of pride rolled down his cheeks. He addressed the assembled officers and men thus: "Here is the Argentine flag. And with all due respect to Great Britain and its people, they will have to understand that the world has changed and certain things of the past cannot come back." He was a model of Latin military courtesy but the message was unmistakable. His soldiers, he said, were ready in case of attack, though he added: "Materially nothing is impregnable. But these islands are spiritually impregnable."

The visit to Washington by Mr Pym was also something of an exercise in public relations, planned to make an impression upon the Americans. It was three weeks since the invasion, and the dramas of the Haig fly-around mission had begun to draw full attention from American opinion which at first had taken little interest in the crisis. More pressing matters in the US, such as President Reagan's budget, occupied American minds. But Mr Pym's constant reiteration on TV screens that Britain would not shrink from using force if necessary and that it was foolish to believe otherwise, had its effect. After he left, the pro-British lobby in Washington began mustering its supporters. For the first time signs emerged that the American Congress was becoming impatient with the original "even-handed approach" of the White House. The timely recapture of South Georgia demonstrated that Mrs Thatcher meant business, and that events might now be dictated by a fleet in being as much as by diplomacy.

Mr Costa Mendez, the Argentine Foreign Minister, also flew to Washington. His mission was two-fold. He had to be seen talking to Mr Haig, but he also needed to get the Organisation of American States to stick by Argentina, and to provide material support. He was only partially successful. There was a great deal of vociferous rhetoric expounded by the OAS for Argentina, in the cause of Hispanic Solidarity. The Organisation was in favour of a truce, endorsed Argentina's claim to sovereignty over the *Malvinas* and deplored Common Market sanctions against a fellow member. But far from pressing for retaliatory sanctions of their own against Britain, the South American Foreign Ministers declared the crisis should be resolved within the framework of the United Nations Security Council resolution, which called for Argentina to withdraw its troops from the islands. Argentina got half a loaf. It had a rightful claim to the islands but it should not have taken them by force.

From his meetings with Mr Haig at the end of April, the Argentine Foreign Minister emerged with a document bearing the State Department's imprint. Stripped to essentials, it proposed staggering the withdrawal of the Argentine troops and the British task force, the declaration of a demilitarised zone around the Falklands, a five-year tripartite administration, dual nationality for the islanders and a compensation scheme for anyone who wished to leave.

However, the document fudged the fundamental issue by noting that Britain would not be required to recognise Argentine sovereignty. Pressed for his reaction to the proposals, Mr Costa Mendez answered that they would be studied carefully because "we are ready to negotiate, negotiate, negotiate." The State Department said that there was no ultimatum and no deadline for a response to them. They might not be the final proposals but they could help to provide other ideas. But it did not take long for the junta to tell the United States that the document was unsatisfactory and needed some clarification. It was a tactic to buy time, but Britain had no other choice but to continue the negotiating process, and Mr Pym returned to Washington on 1 May.

The time appeared to be right for Mr Pym's return as by now President Regan was ready to announce that he was no longer an umpire but a supporter of Britain. He declared that Britain was America's "closest ally" and, now that the Argentine government had refused to accept a compromise, he was ready to speak of them as aggressors.

Although the President made it clear that there would be no American involvement in any fighting, he was ready to give to the British any military equipment which they might ask for. From that time onwards the export of all military materiel to Argentina was to be suspended and certification of eligibility for military sales was to be withheld. In the economic field the President ordered that new export-import bank credits and guarantees should be suspended and so were commodity credit corporation guarantees.

This development was exactly what Mrs Thatcher had been hoping for: the backing of an old friend at a critical moment. Within hours the total blockade of the area around the Falklands was to come into effect and naval action was imminent. American support not only boosted morale, it also facilitated the full use of Ascension Island.

Ever since the disastrous experience of Sir Anthony Eden during the Suez Crisis of 1956, British governments have been haunted by the consequences of making war without American support. In the Suez operation John Foster Dulles, the then Secretary of State, did everything in his power to prevent and impede. At last Mrs Thatcher's government had the powerful sponsor it needed before the conflict could be put to the test of war.

At the United Nations in New York Mr Pym seemed to be growing in confidence and he began taking a keener interest in the three-point plan which had been drafted by the United States and Peru soon after his arrival. Peru had now come forward as a mediating nation, using its position as a Latin American power to attempt to keep in play the original efforts of Mr Haig.

It was at this stage that naval action in the South Atlantic impinged upon the diplomatic processes. The sinking of the Argentine cruiser, *General Belgrano*, on 2 May, with the loss of 300 seamen, came as a great shock in Washington as well as in London and Buenos Aires. There was a tendency in the United States to see the British fleet as a powerful bullying force, and if it continued sinking ships with such loss of life then public opinion would be outraged. Paradoxically the more successful the British were in naval operations the more it cost the government in terms of support from friends and allies. However, the fortunes of war are rarely predictable and just as indignation was mounting about the killing of Argentine sailors, the Royal Navy suffered its first loss when an Exocet missile put HMS *Sheffield* out of action. In a curious way this seemed to redress the balance. It also increased awareness of the spreading conflict and brought a new sense of urgency to the peace processes.

The immediate effect of the two tragedies was to strengthen the role of the United Nations in the negotiations. Its Secretary General, Mr Javier Perez de Cuellar, a sixty-two-year-old Peruvian diplomat of great experience, was now charged with the task of preventing open war from spreading in the South Atlantic. He had held office for five months at the UN and was already familiar with its ways. He had served as its special representative in Cyprus, had dealt with the Soviet Union over the invasion of Afghanistan and was the chief observer for the organisation during the Zimbabwe elections. Before that he had served his country as a diplomat in a number of important capitals.

In 1981, after a long struggle over the appointment of the new Secretary General to replace Dr Kurt Waldheim, he had been chosen finally as a compromise candidate. Mr Perez de Cuellar is a more popular figure at UN headquarters than his predecessor and has a reputation for being less remote. Tall and scholarly, more of a thinker than a talker, he had been quietly building up his own small "task force" for dealing with the Falklands crisis. He had not been keen, however, to push himself forward too early as a negotiator or mediator, contrary to the belief of Labour Party leaders in London.

The earlier Peruvian proposals, which were endorsed by Washington, consisted of three main points. These were a ceasefire followed by the withdrawal of military forces, the withdrawal to be supervised by the United States, Peru and two other countries; and the start of Anglo–Argentine talks without preconditions but with a deadline running into early next year.

Argentine intransigence quickly killed off that plan. President Galtieri said the proposals resembled too closely similar ones put forward by Mr Haig. The sinking of the *Belgrano* was quoted as an "aggravating factor". In fact the junta was in no mood to consider withdrawing its forces, and it was certainly not prepared to give up claims to sovereignty.

The United Nations' proposals – which Mr Perez de
Cuellar liked to call "ideas" – were linked to the American
and Peruvian plan. Thus they involved an immediate ceasefire and simultaneous withdrawal of forces, but with a
United Nations involvement thereafter followed by negotiations on the island's final status.

From the beginning it was not easy for Mrs Thatcher and
her "War Cabinet" to have much confidence in Mr Perez de
Cuellar's ideas. After all, the UN had a poor record in
dealing promptly and efficiently with the crisis that had been
dumped into its lap several times over the years. It was feared
in London that while the UN talked, the Argentines would
dig deeper and deeper into their foxholes on the Falklands,
and the sea around the islands would become rougher and
the weather dirtier.

There had been precious little evidence in the month or so
since the invasion to indicate the junta's willingness to meet
the demands of UN Security Council Resolution 502. A case
in point was the Argentine leadership's trick of contradicting
itself. Sometimes Mr Costa Mendez seemed determined to
be all things to all men. Frequently he appeared unable to
obtain the junta's backing for decisions he had already
approved in Washington. On 2 May an official Argentine
note to the State Department said the American proposals
had not been rejected. Four days later Mr Costa Mendez
stated flatly that they had been, and added that of course
Argentina had not wanted the world to think it was unwilling
to sit down and talk about peace.

But Mr Perez de Cuellar did not give up. In his room on
the thirty-eighth floor of the UN headquarters on New
York's East River, he went over and over the Haig and
Peruvian proposals with Sir Anthony Parsons, the British
UN representative, and Mr Enrique Ros, the Argentine
Under Secretary for Foreign Affairs. The talks proceeded in
fits of pessimism and starts of something akin to hope. Sir
Anthony's stock line to waiting journalists was: "We are still
in business." The Argentine preferred to say: "I am bringing
back some interesting answers." Mr Perez de Cuellar re-

peatedly emphasised that the talks were at a crucial state.

He was bringing into play the so-called Kissinger, or jigsaw puzzle approach to peace-making by taking the negotiations slowly and stage by stage. First, the Secretary General seized on the "easy" pieces on which there was no disagreement, and fitted them into place. They could then be removed to be pressed into the jigsaw at the very last moment. The really "hard" pieces, in this case the question of sovereignty, were left until last, when the two sides felt compelled to finish the jigsaw because they had come so far already.

By Friday, 14 May, substantial progress had been made in the diplomatic exchanges. Both sides had agreed that a ceasefire would be linked to a phased and supervised disengagement of forces. There was still some dispute about how far the British task force – which had proved to be Britain's key card, as intended – would need to withdraw. After all, the Argentine troops would be withdrawing only some 350 miles to their mainland bases. But Britain had dropped its earlier demand that there could be no ceasefire until the Argentine troops had packed up their equipment and cleared off home.

Mr Perez de Cuellar was also trying to find agreement on the form of the interim administration of the islands while talks about their future were taking place. Could Anglo-Argentine joint control work? Apparently not. Would it be better if it were undertaken by three or four other countries such as West Germany, Peru and the United States? Just possibly. Or was the best idea of all a United Nations trustee arrangement? And if so what form would it take?

Britain was showing some flexibility, or, as Mr Pym put it, "a careful balance of firmness in the essential principles, tempered by the necessary measure of readiness to negotiate on issues where negotiation was possible". The junta too, during the crucial second week in May appeared to be softening the line, or at least toning down the demagogic harangues. It had been insisting Britain should commit itself to ceding sovereignty before peace negotiations. Britain had been saying just as firmly that it rejected such a course.

The junta's problem was clear enough and of its own making. It wanted to be able to justify both the 2 April invasion, and the withdrawal, by being able to claim Britain had conceded Argentine sovereignty even if talks would have to be held on the issue. Mr Costa Mendez gave the first signs of Argentine flexibility by saying on American television "we are not saying Britain must accept at the beginning our sovereignty . . . We are not putting sovereignty as a precondition for talks." President Galtieri appeared to support his Foreign Minister by saying: "We are not going to renounce sovereignty but we can talk to reach the goal." Then he added: "Although not for another 149 years." Once again, though, he made it hard for Britain to feel confident about entering into any agreement with the junta. In the very next interview he gave he said, "Argentines, Latin Americans and Peruvians know that the *Malvinas* Islands have been, are, and will be Argentine. This issue is not under discussion."

Sir Anthony Parsons, and Britain's other key representative in the United States, Sir Nicholas Henderson, the Ambassador, flew to London on Friday, 14 May, to give the government their assessment of Mr Perez de Cuellar's initiative, and to state their opinion as to whether it had any hope of ultimate success. While they were in the air British troops were landing on Pebble Island off the northern tip of West Falkland. They blew up an ammunition dump, and destroyed eleven Argentine aircraft on the grass landing strip. That weekend was the seventh that the Falkland Islanders had spent under Argentine occupation. The British government made it clear there was going to be no sell-out of fundamental objectives: the complete withdrawal of Argentine forces and the restored rights of the islanders to decide their own future. Mrs Thatcher said it clearly at a Scottish Conservative rally, and her argument was echoed elsewhere by Mr Pym, Mr Nott and other ministers.

President Galtieri was also in a pessimistic, and tough, mood. He committed Argentina to fighting the South Atlantic war to the bloody end, claiming, "If it is necessary in order to safeguard the reasonable pride – the historical pride – of Argentina and of Latin America we are ready to lose 4,000 or 40,000 people in five or six months or five or six years."

Even Mr Perez de Cuellar was beginning to sound more and more gloomy about the prospects for his peace plan. He had talks with Sir Anthony Parsons, and with the Argentine Ambassador. He had telephone conversations with both Mrs Thatcher and President Galtieri, and on Wednesday, 19 May, he compared the situation to that of a patient "in intensive care but still alive." Asked to comment on the Secretary General's remark, Sir Anthony Parsons said: "The patient died. It is now either a question of getting a new patient onto the operating table, or a resurrection of the dead."

It was an accurate reflection of the mood in Whitehall. The War Cabinet had no doubts now that the Argentines had been playing for time. The prevarication at the United Nations was further evidence. There was concern too that the resounding support for Britain immediately following the 2 April invasion was beginning to melt away. The Common Market had agreed to extend economic sanctions against Argentina for only a week. There was the prospect of growing opposition to Britain in the United Nations. The task force was unable to enforce a strict blockade. Britain appeared to be losing the propaganda war.

Before a hushed House of Commons Mrs Thatcher spelled out in the fullest detail the government's efforts to achieve a peaceful negotiated settlement of the Falklands dispute, and how the Argentines had turned them down flat. Britain had presented seven sets of peace proposals since the passing of Resolution 502 in the United Nations Security Council. A final nine-point plan – "the farthest that Britain could go" – had not only been rejected, but President Galtieri had also hardened his position. Britain had offered to withdraw the fleet 150 miles from the islands in a bid to win peace. The Argentines wanted both sides to pull back forces to their own countries and for the Royal Marines to leave recaptured South Georgia. There were other sticking points. The Argentines wanted free access for all their citizens to the islands, and refused to enter any talks which did not start on the basis that the Falklands belonged to them. Crucially, the junta would not accept that the interim arrangements should last until agreement was reached about the island's long-term future.

Mrs Thatcher accused General Galtieri of "obduracy, delay, deception and bad faith". She said: "One is bound to ask whether the junta ever intended to seek a peaceful settlement or merely to confuse and prolong the negotiations while remaining in illegal possession of the islands."

Britain had a just cause, she said, but after seven weeks of talks it had finally lost patience. By and large the Commons agreed, although a bitter quarrel erupted in the Labour Party with Mr Foot accusing Mr Benn of stabbing in the back "those who are being sent into battle".

It was clear to the Commons, and to the country, that Thursday, 20 May, was the turning point, and that the task force had been ordered to get on with the job of recapturing the Falkland Islands.

17

THE BATTLE UP TO 20 MAY, 1982

The realities of modern war came to the Falklands before dawn on 1 May when a solitary Vulcan bomber of the RAF dropped its bombs across the runway of Stanley airport. It was a remarkable feat of airmanship for the Vulcan to have got to the Falklands at all, for it had flown 3,500 miles from Ascension Island on a mission which entailed a fifteen-hour round trip. During the flight it was refuelled three times in the air by Victor tankers drawn from 55 and 57 Squadrons deployed to Ascension Island from their home base at RAF Marham in Norfolk. It amounted to more than just a bombing raid on an airfield, and was an indication to the Argentines that even their airfields on the mainland were not outside the reach of the RAF. The Vulcan's stealthy high-altitude sortie, which probably gave the Argentines no warning until the bombs began to crash around them, was followed with an attack on the airfield and grass airstrip at Goose Green by what the Defence Ministry described as "a substantial number" of Sea Harriers. This was a more conventional attack with the Harriers screaming across the sky, dropping their bombs and straffing the airfields while the defenders "hosepiped" the sky with automatic anti-aircraft guns. Despite the intensity of the flak however, only one plane was damaged – by a single bullet.

Later the same afternoon ships of the task force closed in on the islands and pounded the airfield at Stanley with their 4.5 guns to "reinforce the effects of the bombing and to deter repair work". It was during this bombardment that the Argentines took their first counter-action, sending over a force of their Israeli-built Daggers – a version of the French

Mirage ground attack aircraft. They were picked up by the fleet's radar and the Sea Harriers took off to intercept them. Two of the Daggers were "splashed" and another shot down by its own side's anti-aircraft fire. And when a flight of Argentine Canberra bombers took up the challenge later in the evening, a further Dagger was shot down and another damaged. It was during this last engagement that the frigate HMS *Arrow* was hit by splinters and the task force suffered another war casualty, Able Seaman Ian Britnell, a gunner on a missile battery, who was hit in the chest by shrapnel and seriously wounded.

The first blood had been drawn on both sides in the battle for the recapture of the Falklands and the propaganda machines in London and Buenos Aires went into action in styles which were to set the pattern of this particular aspect of the battle. In London, the Defence Ministry spokesman, Mr Ian McDonald, read out the low-key British version of the action in his slow, prim voice, insisting that "in the last twenty-four hours we have lost no aircraft, fixed wing or helicopters". In Buenos Aires the reaction was something less than low key with tales of the Sea Harriers being virtually wiped out, large-scale landings being repulsed and the *Hermes* being set on fire. A more certain loss was that of Governor Rex Hunt's newly-acquired Cessna light aircraft which "was sitting beside the main hangar at the airport. The bombers may have destroyed it, and I'm sure the insurance won't cover the cost."

More poignantly, RAF Flight Lieutenant Bertie Penfold, flying from *Hermes*, told how he had shot down a Dagger which had fired a missile at another Harrier. "The Harrier accompanying me broke away from the missiles and I was able to turn up and into the enemy. I locked a Sidewinder into his jet wake and after three or four seconds the missile hit. There was an enormous explosion and I felt quite sick. Being a pilot myself it was sad to see an aircraft explode. But it's got to be done."

What eventually emerged from this opening round was that the Argentine claims about British losses were fictional

but that they were correct in asserting that the airfield at
Stanley had not been knocked out. Heavily damaged yes, but
not put out of action. It could still be used by aircraft with
short take-off and landing capabilities. And if the British
wanted to draw the noose of their blockade tight they would
have to keep on attacking the runway.

However, while the lessons of the raids were being
absorbed, the impact of this first round of fighting was
completely overshadowed by the sinking of the Argentine
cruiser *General Belgrano* by torpedoes from the nuclear
powered hunter-killer submarine *Conqueror*.

The 13,645 ton cruiser had survived a remarkable career.
Commissioned in 1939 as the United States Navy's *Phoenix*,
she had come through the Japanese attack on Pearl Harbor
unscathed. She took part in several naval encounters during
the Second World War and was sold to Argentina in 1951 for
7.8 million dollars. Radically rebuilt for her new owners, she
had missile launchers and helicopter landing pads added to
complement her fifteen 6-inch guns – the largest guns on any
ship in the South Atlantic. On the day her luck ran out she
was being escorted by two destroyers armed with Exocet
missiles, whose air-launched version were soon to prove their
potency. But once the order to attack had been given to the
Conqueror, which had been shadowing this group as it skirted
the edge of the total exclusion zone, the *Belgrano* stood no
chance. The *Conqueror* had been designed to hunt and kill
ships as well as Russian missile submarines and it is one of
the world's most powerful battle-ships. She can circumnavi-
gate the world without resurfacing, running at a constant
thirty knots and has six torpedo tubes for her mix of Mark 8
and Tigerfish torpedoes. The Mark 8s are straight running,
salvo-fired short range weapons of old design but with a very
high explosive punch. The modern Tigerfish is a weapon of
the missile age, which is guided towards its target by wires
from the submarine from as far as twenty miles away. When
the target comes within range of the torpedo's own sonar, a
computer built into the torpedo takes over and controls its
final run to the target. The high explosive warhead of several

hundred pounds can be set to detonate on impact, or its proximity fuse will set it off when it comes within destructive range of its victim. The Tigerfish is a deadly weapon which rarely misses. It cannot afford to. Each torpedo costs £300,000. It seems almost certain it was a Mark 8 that sank the *Belgrano*. Nevertheless, the British were happy to let the Argentines think their cruiser had been sunk by some super weapon in order to encourage the rest of the Navy to stay in port.

Whichever torpedoes were fired at the *General Belgrano* they ran straight and true. The cruiser, which had seen so many desperate actions in the Second World War, heeled over and sank without firing a shot in this mini-war. Some 300 men were lost.

On the same day another new British weapon was blooded. Sea Skua missiles fired from Lynx helicopters sank the armed tug *Comodoro Somellera* and badly damaged her sister ship, the *Alferez Sobral* after they had fired on a sub-marine-hunting Sea King helicopter. These successes for the task force had a strange effect in Britain as well as the rest of the world. The feeling grew that the Argentines were out-matched, that the British could defeat their soldiers, knock their planes out of the sky and sink their ships without them being able to strike back. While acknowledging that the Argentines were the aggressors it seemed that possibly Britain was going too far in teaching them a lesson and there was disquiet as the *General Belgrano* had been attacked out-side the total exclusion zone. Even the explanation that the cruiser, with its attendant Exocet destroyers, was closing on advanced units of the task force did not erase the disquiet. Neither did the added explanation that there was another zone, a "defence area" round the ships of the task force which could overlap the total exclusion zone.

It seemed to many that the British were being unfair. It was an attitude which infuriated those who knew the Argen-tines' military strength and appreciated the determination with which they would defend the *Islas Malvinas*. It was as if the British would have to take some casualties before it was appreciated that we were engaged in a war with both sides possessing weapons of enormous power.

That realisation came to the British nation in the cruellest of ways on Tuesday, 4 May, when HMS *Sheffield*, the "Shiny Sheff", commanded by Captain James "Sam" Salt, was destroyed by an Exocet missile, launched by a Super Etendard naval strike aircraft, and twenty of her crew were killed. The men were mourned but what shocked Britons even more was that one of the Royal Navy's destroyers could be wiped out by a pilot who released his missile twenty miles away after seeing the ship merely as a blip on his radar and who returned home without knowing what he had done.

Two Exocets, whose name comes from Exocoetus, a type of flying fish which darts over the waves at high speed, had been launched. One missed its target, possibly turned off course by the fleet's electronic counter-measures, but the other struck the *Sheffield* at nearly the speed of sound and tore a gaping hole in her side some six feet above the water level before exploding in the control room, the heart of the ship. The kinetic energy of the missile striking and the ship and the unused rocket fuel in the missile started fires and the explosion of the warhead spread the flames.

Captain Salt had only twenty seconds' warning of the approach of the missile. This left him no time to fire the "chaff", a cloud of aluminium strips designed to confuse the missile's guidance system, and the missile was fired from so far away at such low level that the long-range Sea Dart anti-aircraft system did not even pick up the Super Etendards as their pilots pressed the button and turned for home. "We only had time to say 'Take Cover'," said Captain Salt, "then it hit us. It had a devastating effect. It hit the centre of the ship, the centre of all operations, mechanical, detection, weaponry.

"You could feel the heat of the deck beneath your feet. The fire spread along the ship and exploded outwards and upwards. It took fifteen to twenty seconds – that might sound incredible – before the whole working area of the ship was engulfed by steaming black acrid smoke. The area round where the missile penetrated was glowing red . . . it was white-hot then red-hot.''

The *Sheffield* lost power. There were no lights, no pressure in the fire-fighters' hoses. And nobody could reach the control room or the galley beneath it to bring out anybody who might have survived.

The struggle to save the *Sheffield* went on for five hours, with other ships sending their fire-fighting teams. But the destroyer was completely blotted out from the sight of the rest of the fleet by the smoke which formed a solid column from the sea to the clouds.

Afterwards, Captain Salt was full of praise for his crew: "The men were quite incredible. I have no doubt that the ship's company really saved themselves by their own sensible efforts. I'm sure that every captain would say that his ship's company was the best, but I know mine is." Reluctantly, when there was danger of the flames reaching the magazine where the Sea Dart warheads were stored, he gave the decision to abandon ship. Everybody who had survived the fires was saved. The crew of twenty-one officers and 249 ratings were indeed fortunate in that only twenty of them died in such a devastating incident but it brought home to Britain that when a nation embarks on military action a price in lives must always be paid. The mourning bells tolled in Sheffield and also at Portsmouth where the destroyer had been based.

The naval implications of the destruction of the *Sheffield* became a matter for public concern. Soon everyone who read the newspapers or watched television knew what naval experts had known for a number of years: that the Type 42 destroyers were good sea ships but were underweaponed. Their two Sea Dart long-range anti-aircraft missile launchers are effective against aircraft attacks from above 1,000 feet but cannot cope with missiles such as the Exocet, travelling at nearly the speed of sound just over the wave tops where "clutter" from the sea confuses the defensive system's radar. Also with only two launchers, the Type 42s would be in difficulties against a number of attacks launched by aircraft coming in from different angles. The answer to the Exocet is known. It is the new lightweight version of the Sea Wolf anti-missile missile. But the Type 42 cannot accommodate the Sea Wolf, not only because it is too "compact" for the radars and computers which control the Sea Wolf system which are the size of a house, but also because it does not have the waterline to allow the fitting of the system. This revelation was followed by the news that even the *Broadsword* and *Brilliant*, the Type 22 frigates and the only ships with the task force equipped with the Sea Wolf, do not have the lightweight version guided by the new radar that is needed to enable the missile to destroy sea-skimmers such as Exocet.

The Sea Wolf system which is fitted to the frigates is deadly against aircraft at close range and against missiles flying above the radar interference caused by reflections from the sea surface. With a range of three and a half miles and travelling at twice the speed of sound, it can shoot down a 4.5 inch shell in mid flight. But it cannot be certain of hitting the much larger Exocet jinking its way over the tops of the waves. And the new version, with its Marconi "anti-clutter" radar will not be ready for at least another two years. If an already developed Dutch radar system had been adopted for the Sea Wolf, it is possible that it would have been ready for service now but for what at the time seemed sound economic reasons it was decided to develop Britain's own system. Such thinking, when set against the £120 million cost of a modern warship must now be questioned. It was especially unfortunate for the task force in which every ship was now shown to be at risk from Exocets, but then nobody had really envisaged going to war in the South Atlantic against an enemy using missiles which were virtually the monopoly of the West. When the order for the Sea Wolf was placed and the completion date decided, it was done on the assumption that the Russians had not yet reached a dangerous point in their development of sea-skimmers and, so the thinking ran, they were the only people we were likely to go to war with.

The abandoned *Sheffield* defied the fires raging in her and with the seas uncharacteristically calm, remained afloat while the flames gutted her. Later, Captain Salt reboarded her with damage parties and she was taken in tow, with missile experts waiting anxiously to examine the damage caused by the Exocet. But the sea got up and, as if tired of it all, she rolled over. The waves poured through the great rend in her side and she sank to become an official war grave for all the men who died in her.

The destruction of the *Sheffield* saw the end of the feeling that the British were being unfair to the "Argies" and more sober assessments of the situation were made. It was immediately apparent that with the dwindling force of Harriers – one from 809 Squadron on *Hermes* had been shot down over Goose Green on the same day that the *Sheffield* had been hit and two from 801 Squadron on *Invincible* disappeared two days later, almost certainly after colliding in bad weather – Rear Admiral Woodward would have a hard job defending his fleet against determined attacks, let alone maintaining air supremacy over a beach-head. There was anxious consultation with France over how many Super Etendards and airborne AM39 Exocets had been supplied to the Argentines before their export was banned and *Broadsword* and *Brilliant* took up the advanced radar picket warning role. They at least had a chance of shooting down an Exocet.

At the same time the task force commander, a specialist submariner, became increasingly worried about the non-appearance of Argentina's three remaining submarines.

These submarines, all of them diesel-electric powered, do not compare with Britain's 4,900 ton nuclear-powered monsters. But at first it was felt that the *Santiago del Estro*, sister ship of the captured *Santa Fé*, could, with its long range of 10,000 miles, pose a considerable threat to the *Canberra* or the *Queen Elizabeth II* as they made their way south from Ascension Island loaded with troops and materiel. But then intelligence reports showed that she was laid up in dock, unfit for service and had probably been cannibalised to keep the *Santa Fé* at sea. What did enrage the Navy however, was the way in which the crew of the *Santa Fé* were rapidly returned to Argentina. It was all very well returning a few Marines, they could make no difference to the course of the conflict, but to give the Argentines back a fully trained crew of submarine specialists seemed the height of folly.

The other two submarines are of a different class. German built T209 types, the *Salta* and the *San Luis* are only ten years old and are equipped with modern devices. Their drawback is that they have a limited range and the Argentine Navy did not want them, preferring the British designed Oberon class which are also diesel electric but have an endurance of 9,000 miles. However, the Navy was overruled by the politicians who thought more of the German design's twenty-knot speed under water than the Oberon's endurance. This may well turn out to be a happy decision for Britain. Nevertheless these submarines have another quality which made life difficult for the British fleet. They are very quiet and are not easily detected on the task force's sonar screens. It was believed that at least one of them was hiding in one of the many inlets along the Falkland coast, lying on the sea bed before coming up for air at night and waiting for orders to attack one of the carriers. Undoubtedly a suicide mission, but the captain might judge it worthwhile if he were able to sink *Hermes* or *Invincible*.

The first strictly military reaction to the destruction of the *Sheffield* was to point out that the only way to protect the fleet from such attacks was to knock out the launch aircraft and their bases. This would have involved bombing attacks on airfields on the mainland and a huge air-refuelling operation to get a sufficient number of Vulcans to their targets. The military and political hazards of such an enterprise ruled it out of court. Instead Britain extended the exclusion zone to twelve miles from the Argentine coast, warning that any Argentine ship or aircraft which transgressed would be "dealt with accordingly".

The task force settled down to its blockade, determined to isolate the garrison by sea and air and erode its morale in preparation for the British assault. It is an aspect of naval warfare perfected by the Royal Navy during the Napoleonic Wars.

Another Vulcan flew the long, lonely route from Ascension Island to bomb the runway at Stanley and a group of Harriers used the same in-flight refuelling technique to fly all the 3,400 miles to Ascension Island from Britain in nine hours. It was a feat of navigation and stamina by the pilots, cramped in their small cockpits, and while secrecy was imposed on the rest of the operation, it was believed that some of the Harriers flew the Vulcan route, again refuelling in mid-air, to replace the three Harriers lost by the fleet. The remainder were loaded on to the *Atlantic Conveyor* and sailed south, ready for the landings which most people with the task force and the back-up fleet now believed to be inevitable. Certainly the Harrier pilots needed some help. Flying whenever the weather allowed, they maintained defence patrols over the fleet and hammered at targets on the Falklands, returning again and again to bomb the runway at the airfield. The helicopter pilots also maintained a gruelling schedule of flying in all their various roles.

On Sunday 9 May, two Sea Harriers attacked an Argentine fishing vessel, the *Narwal*, which was straffed and holed by a bomb. The crew surrendered to a boarding party sent by a Sea King helicopter. One man was killed and thirteen injured and the Argentines accused the British pilots of machine-gunning the crew as they abandoned the ship and took to their life rafts. The *Narwal*, they claimed, was an innocent fishing vessel. However, when the boarding party searched the sinking ship they found two naval officers on board and papers which proved that the *Narwal* had been commandeered to form part of a network of fishing boats spying on the task force. One captured document read: "Mission –
To conduct reconnaissance in the assigned zone. Detect and report the position of British air, surface and submarine units. . . . You are to pursue innocent navigation and tasks. On making detection, report in accordance with instructions. If boarded and searched, resistance is not to be made and the

fishing certificate is to be shown." The crew were taken by
helicopter to ships of the task force and the *Narwal* sank the
next day.

Argentine Mirages were chased away. . . . A Puma helicopter was shot down by British aircraft over Stanley. . . .
Frigates bombarded targets on the island. . . . On Tuesday,
11 May, a British frigate, believed to be *Alacrity*, ventured
into the narrow channel between the East and West Falklands. She fired tracer rounds and star shells and put up her
Lynx helicopter while she nosed in and out of the rocky coast
looking for signs of the Argentines. Then she spotted a ship
which tried to run from her. The *Alacrity* fired several quick
shots from her 4.5 gun. They struck home and the ship
exploded in an enormous fireball. The Argentines later
admitted that they had lost contact with one of their supply
ships, the *Islas de Los Estados*. It had become obvious that
under cover of the bad weather, supplies were being brought
in by light aircraft landing on the score of grass airstrips
which dot the Falklands and were then being ferried to
isolated positions by ships sailing at night and taking cover
during the day. Rear Admiral Woodward determined to shut
off all the boltholes.

The following day the Argentines came out for revenge,
and this was the day the Sea Wolf proved itself – at least
against aircraft. Two British ships, one of them either the
Broadsword or the *Brilliant*, were attacked by Skyhawk fighter
bombers, flying low to escape the Sea Dart anti-aircraft
missiles. But the Sea Wolf locked on to them automatically
and when they came within range two were knocked out of
the sky and another dived into the sea trying to avoid a Sea
Wolf.

However, despite this success, one of the frigates was lucky
to be afloat after an attack by a fourth Skyhawk which left her
with a hole through her bows. The Skyhawk scored a direct
hit with a bomb which tore almost horizontally through her
plating, failed to explode and disappeared through the other
side of the ship. It caused no casualties and the frigate was
soon repaired with the facilities available on the aircraft

carriers and support ships. It was an incident which demonstrated that despite the success of the Sea Wolf the British
ships were still vulnerable to a determined attack by brave
pilots, especially from low-flying strike aircraft, even the
ageing, second-hand Skyhawks flown at the limit of their
range. They could be "splashed" by the Harriers but even
with the arrival of all the reinforcements there were still only
about forty Harriers and they were having difficulties with
the weather. To land a Harrier on the deck of a small carrier
pitching in a South Atlantic winter sea is tremendously
difficult. The Skyhawk pilots had the comforting knowledge
that they were flying home to solid land with proper run-
ways. However, General Lami Dozo, chief of the Argentine
Air Force as well as being a member of the junta, used his
aircraft sparingly. He was saving them for "D-Day" when,
he said, he would launch a "massive attack" on the British
fleet.

The attack by the Skyhawks, however, confirmed suspicions that the Argentines were being directed to their targets
by mobile radars operating from the Falklands. These became a priority target.

On Friday, 14 May, the British made their first land attack
on the Falklands. It was a harassing raid designed to erode
the Argentine soldiers' morale, to take out some potentially
dangerous aircraft and to destroy a particularly troublesome
radar on Pebble Island, lying off the northern coast of West
Falkland. The raiding party was landed by helicopter some
three miles from its objective, the island's grass airstrip. This
had become the main conduit for supplies reaching the
beleaguered Argentine forces by light aircraft slipping across
from the mainland. Their faces blacked, the raiders made
their way across the rugged country undetected. They had a
gunnery officer with them and when they were in position he
called down fire from ships which closed into the shore. The
quick-firing 4.5s are deadly accurate and great care was
taken not to hit the civilian settlement of Falklanders near the
airstrip. Brian Hanrahan of the BBC, who was on board one
of the destroyers taking part in the bombardment, said in his

dispatch: "The bulk of the island, black against a luminous sky, was suddenly lit up by star shells and red tracer lines which climbed lazily towards the Argentine positions. From the sea the ships threw out orange flames and covering fire, more star shells to show the attacking force the ground then salvo after salvo of high explosive, each shell whining away into the darkness, twenty at a time, one shell every two seconds."

When the barrage lifted, the raiders split into two parties, one firing long bursts of automatic fire at the Argentines' positions, forcing them to keep their heads down, and the other splitting into smaller groups each with their own targets, moving across the airstrip, destroying aircraft and those installations left undamaged by the shell fire. And of course, the radar. "It was very much a priority for them to put them in and for us to take them out," said a task force spokesman after the raid.

At first it was thought that the raiders were Marines but in its planning and execution it bore all the hallmarks of the Special Air Service and some days after the raid it became known that it had been carried out by forty-eight members of the 22nd Regiment SAS working in their usual four-man "sticks".

The SAS started its life in 1941 when Colonel David Stirling formed it to strike behind Rommel's lines in the Western Desert. His band of very tough, dedicated soldiers perfected the technique of driving through the desert for days to reach German airfields where "sticks" would blow up aircraft parked on the ground while the trucks, bristling with automatic weapons, would career round the field shooting up whatever they could find. The SAS has become much more sophisticated; it is regarded as the best anti-terrorist unit anywhere in the world and it has at its command a variety of electronic equipment. But, apart from the use of helicopters instead of trucks, their raid on Pebble Island was a classic operation straight out of their regimental textbook: get in quick, do as much damage as possible, frighten the enemy and disappear.

They had a busy night, destroying six Pucara ground attack aircraft, one Short Skyvan transport and five other light aircraft. The destruction of the Pucaras was particularly satisfying because these are the slow but tough and heavily armed anti-insurgency planes, used with such effect against the ERP guerrillas in Argentina's wild interior, and they could have been an embarrassment to a landing force. The SAS slipped away, leaving the wreckage blazing, with just two minor casualties. The task force commander was pleased to receive their report that the Argentine soldiers did not show much taste for battle.

Sandy Woodward's policy of demoralisation and strangulation was working out: keep the sea clear of Argentine ships and the air clear of Argentine planes. Strike at targets which threaten the safety of the task force. Harass the soldiers, most of them young conscripts already suffering from the effects of the Falklands winter. Do as much damage as possible, wear down the enemy's morale while avoiding losses until the main force arrives and the order is given to go in.

Meanwhile those main forces were continuing to increase in size and strength. The Sea Wolf-equipped frigate *Battleaxe* joined her sister ships and the destroyer *Exeter*, descendant of that other *Exeter* which had limped into the Falklands after its epic battle with the *Graf Spee*, sailed to take the place of her sister ship *Sheffield*. More ships were requisitioned. The car ferry *St Edmund*, the container ship *Bezant*, the tankers *Alvega* and *Balder* and the freighter *Scottish Eagle* were pressed into service and 300 Royal Navy and Royal Marine reservists were warned that they might be called up.

The liner *Canberra* with Marines and Paratroopers and the cavalrymen of the Blues and Royals with their Scorpion light tanks, and other supporting units approached the war zone. The *Queen Elizabeth II*, laden with Guardsmen and Gurkhas, had been given an exuberant send-off from Southampton. The Gurkhas, some of the best fighting soldiers in the world, had arrived last on the quayside and had been greeted with a great roar from the Scots and Welsh Guards already lining the ship's rails.

The stage was set for the invasion. Almost all the players were in position and the world had settled into the auditorium waiting for the most unlikely of dramas to unfold. Would it be farce or tragedy? It waited only on the political decision for the curtain to go up.

A prologue was provided by Captain Christopher Burne, a naval officer on the *Canberra* who circulated a quotation from Clausewitz around the ship: "Everything is very simple in war, but the simplest thing is very difficult. These difficulties accumulate and produce a friction which no man can imagine exactly who has not seen war."

18

THE CRYSTAL BALL

History will show that the Falklands conflict has acted as a remarkable catalyst, bringing about fundamental changes in a number of fields in many parts of the world. In most cases these changes were already in the making. What the conflict has done is to hurry them on, forcing them to emerge months and, in some cases, years before they would have taken their place in the world's order of events.

One such change became inevitable on the very first day of the crisis. The need to gather together a conventional task force meant that Britain's defence policy, based on the purchase of the American Trident ballistic missile system for £7,500 million pounds (to be spent over the next fifteen years, while conventional weapons took second place to the nuclear deterrent), would have to be re-examined in its entirety. The Trident policy had already been attacked not only by anti-nuclear campaigners but also by military men who think it a great mistake to run down Britain's conventional forces in order to pay for the Trident. They have no objection to Trident as a deterrent but argue that the money being spent on it would be better used on conventional arms, particularly on more ships.

As soon as the crisis started, the makeshift fleet had to be put together without a single conventional large aircraft carrier and with ships designed to fight a major war conducted mostly by submarines rather than a local conflict fought out on the surface. This gave the Trident critics their chance to strike. While agreeing that the fleet had been efficiently assembled, they insisted that it had only been

made possible by an accident of timing and that if the
Argentine invasion had been delayed by only a few months, it
would have been impossible to gather the fleet at all. Admiral
of the Fleet, Lord Hill-Norton, writing to *The Times*, put it
this way: "It is certain that had the humiliating seizure of
the Falklands occurred after the Defence Secretary's ill-
conceived intentions had taken effect, no military option
would have been available to the government."

There are others who argue that it does not make sense to
throw away a policy designed to deter the West's only serious
enemy, the Soviet Union, because of an isolated incident
which is unlikely ever to happen again. The rumblings of this
argument have persisted throughout the conflict and
although Mr Nott insists that he will stick to the broad lines
of his policy he has already made one small but significant
concession: HMS *Endurance* has been reprieved. It was the
announcement that she was going to be withdrawn from the
South Atlantic which helped to convince President Galtieri
that Britain would offer no resistance to his invasion. Mr
Nott has also been forced to postpone the publication of the
Defence White Paper for 1982 which would have set out the
government's defence policy based on the purchase of the
Trident. There is no doubt that the White Paper will undergo
drastic revision. Just how drastic the changes will be remains
to be seen but the stage is set for what threatens to be the most
acrimonious defence debate for many years. We could yet see
admirals marching hand in hand with the anti-nuclear
campaigners, crying: "Ban the Trident."

It is not only in Britain that the conflict will cause much
rethinking of defence policies. The United States and the
Soviet Union are watching every aspect of the battle, evalu-
ating tactics and the lessons provided by the use of new
missiles being tried under battle conditions for the first time.
Are big carriers too vulnerable? What can be done about
missiles such as the Exocet? How does the Harrier match up
to conventional aircraft? The answers to these and many
more military questions will bring about fundamental
changes in the armed forces of the super powers. The cost of

missile systems is so enormous and the effect of single missiles
so deadly that they cannot afford to make mistakes.

The debate about Trident is, of course, a matter of money
and the next monetary question looming out of the fog of war
is: will the cost of the Falklands conflict throw the government's economic plans off course?

We have already pointed to the way in which the need to
pay for ships, dockyard work and essential supplies has
forced the government to pump some money into the economy, but it is a limited amount and for a short term. And, on
13 May, in a written answer in the House of Commons, Mr
Brittan, Chief Secretary to the Treasury, assured the House
that expenditure on the Falklands operation has given the
government no reason to modify its forecast that inflation
will be down to nine per cent by the fourth quarter of 1982.

The *Daily Telegraph* loyally supported the government, did
some sums and said that "in these circumstances it is difficult
to envisage how the Falklands will throw the economy off
course. At the worst, interest rate falls may be deferred a few
months and the Chancellor may lose the opportunity of
providing some tax relief this autumn."

But there were others who were not as sanguine.

No one in Whitehall will give any official figures on the cost
of the expedition but one estimate was that it cost £50 million
to get the fleet in position and that the cost of keeping it there
was about £1 million a day. And that was before the shooting
started. With 4.5 inch shells costing £80 each being fired in
salvos of twenty, and anti-aircraft missiles costing between
£7,000 and £11,000 each, the price of a shooting match
escalates rapidly. On top of all that will be the cost of
replacing lost ships and aircraft.

The *Financial Times* sounded a warning, pointing out that
as time goes on attention is likely to centre on the "public
expenditure cost, which is so often underestimated in the
case of overseas expeditions because the repercussions of
decisions taken in the heat of the moment are not foreseen."

Allied to fears for the economy is the certainty of changes
in Britain's business relationships with Argentina. These

have always been strong. Among British-owned firms in Argentina are Duperial, a wholly owned subsidiary of ICI; Cooper (Veterinary Products); Wellcome Argentina; and Glaxo Laboratories (Pharmaceuticals); Unilever; British American Tobacco; Shell; the Bank of London and South America; and Barclay's Bank. There are also three big British ranch-owning companies in Patagonia with head offices in London: Tecka Land Co; Argentine Southern Land Co; and Lochiel Sheep Farming Co. All these came under the financial restrictions on 20 May, prohibiting the sale of all United Kingdom government and private assets in Argentina and it is hardly likely that British companies will any longer enjoy a favoured position in Argentina whatever the outcome of the crisis.

We have already mentioned the other great financial worry: that Argentina will go bankrupt and take some other South American countries with her. Western banks were already beginning to question the wisdom of lending huge amounts of money to countries without applying the same sort of solvency risk tests they would apply to an individual who asks for a loan. The doubts were started by Poland's financial troubles and already there were many who questioned the wisdom of pouring yet more money into weak South American economies. The dangers posed by the Falklands crisis have hastened the rethinking process and it is likely that the banks will be more careful where they lend their money in the future.

The collapse of the Argentine economy would be just one of a number of circumstances which might bring down the junta and bring chaos to Argentina. The junta certainly could not survive defeat and it is unlikely even to survive victory, for what the crisis has brought about is a revival of the political parties. Banned by the junta, political leaders such as Angel Robeldo were allowed to re-enter politics in order to whip up nationalist fever over the *Islas Malvinas*. Robeldo, campaigning for the leadership of the Peronist party, was given licence to say things which would have meant his immediate arrest before 2 April – as long as he encouraged his followers to support the invasion. "We all say yes to battle, yes to sacrifice and yes to obligation," he said in one speech, adding: "But we all want to be able to say yes to decisions. The people cannot be ignored like actors sitting in the audience watching the historic drama unfold in front of them on the stage." Robeldo was allowed to get away with such talk because he appealed for national unity but what he said reveals the depth of the disunity papered over by the Falklands crisis. The disunity exists not only among the people but also among the military leaders themselves. It spreads to the various factions in the Army which will no longer be able to claim the junta's support on the grounds of its anti-Communist stand. Political interest in Argentina is growing: most of the left-wingers have "disappeared" and the opposition now comes from the Peronist trades unions and the parties of the centre, such as the Radicals, Christian Democrats and Peronists, most of whom actually welcomed the military coup in 1976.

At the very heart of the Falklands crisis is the fact that although this dispute over national sovereignty is between Argentina and Britain, it vitally concerns other nations. If President Galtieri were allowed to succeed with his invasion then Guyana, facing territorial demands from Venezuela, and Belize, fearing occupation by Guatemala, would naturally enough feel that the green light had been given to their enemies; the discussions between Spain and the United Kingdom over the future of Gibraltar might be affected; Argentina would feel free to seize the three islands in the Beagle Channel whose ownership it disputes with Chile; Oman and Brunei – independent states protected by British forces – would have cause to look over their shoulders.

But the nation affected the most will be the one that tried the hardest to bring about a peaceful solution – the United States. President Reagan's South American policy was already creaking under the weight of the killings in El Salvador and the effect of high interest rates paid on American loans. But Argentina was still regarded in Washington as a great bastion of anti-Communism in South America.

The friendship of Mrs Jeane Kirkpatrick and General Vernon Walters gave President Galtieri every reason to assume that the United States, if not actually supporting his invasion, would do nothing to hinder him. But he misjudged the American people as much as he misjudged the British because when the chips were down President Reagan had to support Britain, "our closest ally". The result is that not only has the United States lost support in Argentina, it has also lost ground in other Latin American states – Brazil, Peru, Venezuela, Panama – who regard the conflict as the left-over of an ancient era of colonialism, with the United States supporting the imperial power, Britain. It may sound ludicrous for Fidel Castro to ask Colonel Gaddafi to take steps to prevent what he described as a United States-backed British invasion of the Falkland Islands, but the message comes across loud and clear to the Third World: don't trust the United States. The EEC also lost friends in Latin America by imposing sanctions on Argentina. It seemed as if the old colonial world had been called in to attack the rights of the new.

From this stems the certainty that the only country to benefit from the conflict may be the Soviet Union. The Kremlin has played the game very cleverly. It has supported Argentina's claim to the Falklands and it has accused the British of being the aggressors. At the same time it has managed to distance itself from the junta so that when a new government takes power, as it surely will, the Soviet Union will be able to claim they supported the Argentine people but not the junta. They will try to pick up support not only among the Argentines but also among the other Latin American peoples who are disillusioned by American and EEC support for Britain. And Castro's message to Gaddafi must be looked at in this context.

So the effects of the Falklands crisis roll on. In Britain the invasion shattered the Foreign Office. In many respects it was the worst day in its 200 years of existence. Not only did the event lead to the resignation of its leader, Lord Carrington, but it also swept away the two Foreign Office Ministers of State. Perhaps worst of all was that once again the invasion made the Foreign Office appear to the public in such a bad light. It became the scapegoat, the target of abuse and the object of ridicule. At best, according to popular wisdom, British diplomats were mere incompetents. At worst, they were traitors and quislings – after all, it was said, remember Burgess and Maclean, who were always on the look-out for an opportunity to hand over Britain's heritage to foreigners. Yet the Foreign Office can be said to have survived, and remained intact. There were no dismissals, demotions or reshuffles. True, the Permanent Under Secretary, Sir Michael Palliser, retired having reached sixty and only a few days after the debacle, but he was promptly appointed a special adviser on the Falklands to the Prime Minister and attached to the Cabinet Office. The Assistant Under Secretary in charge of the South American Department also stayed on, as did the Head of the Department.

It is a foregone conclusion that the proposed inquiry into the aspects of the Falkland crisis will not be allowed to become a witch-hunt. The intelligence summaries on Argentina's intentions are unlikely to be made public. We will not be told what course of action – if any – individual British diplomats involved in South American affairs were recommending when the Argentines began signalling their intentions earlier this year. The files stamped "Secret", which contain the facts and such comments as "no action called for", will not be produced for public examination.

But was the Foreign Office really at fault? Was it wrong to have become involved in protracted dealings with the Argentines over the Falklands during the last twenty years? Had not the political leaders during that time supported pragmatism, negotiations and even compromise because they realised that the Falklands could not be defended except by exceptional adjustments to Britain's defence and foreign policies? And who was responsible, ultimately, for the decision to scrap HMS *Endurance*, the solitary surface ship kept in the South Atlantic?

The Foreign Office has been overhauled – reformed is too

strong a word – several times since the Suez crisis, in a genuine effort to make it more efficient, realistic, cost-effective, authoritative, and representative. However, although he strenuously denied it at the time of his resignation, Lord Carrington and the Foreign Office clearly ignored the specks on the horizon which have caused so much trouble in the past because they were concentrating on the so-called big issues – the Common Market, East–West relations. Simply, the Foreign Office got it wrong.

The unknown factor in assessing the long-term effects of the crisis upon British politics is how seriously attempts will be made to discover why the Thatcher government allowed itself to be taken by surprise by President Galtieri in the first place. On this question the Opposition will no doubt concentrate its political fire. For even if it is assumed that in the time of danger, the government behaved well and fought back with determination, there can be no doubt that this same government was responsible for the blunder in the first place. The post mortem will provide the contentious issue for a renewed party electoral battle.

In the local government elections held during the crisis, the Conservatives did very well and both the Labour Party and the Social Democratic/Liberal alliance lost ground. As talk of a general election began to be heard, the thought was that perhaps the Tories would try to cash in on a popular mood of national elation which always favours their party. So far as the Labour Party is concerned, as we have seen in an earlier chapter, the crisis served to increase divisions between left and right. It is likely that the conflict may take its toll of SDP/Liberal chances, which had looked so promising only a few months before. Although Dr David Owen, their spokesman on the Falklands conflict, came out of the crisis very well, it was felt that a new party, without the experience of power, could not expect to do well at the polling stations in such times of national peril.

That said, there can be little doubt that the effect of the whole crisis was to bring the nation together in remarkable fashion, and to restore feelings of patriotism and self-confidence. For whatever may be said against nationalism, it has to be admitted that nationhood is a feeling much better understood by citizens than internationalism.

A parallel might be found in the developments in France after the return to power of General de Gaulle in 1958 at a time of national crisis. By providing a strong lead, by reminding the French people of the virtues of courage and loyalty, he created a new and successful France. It is too soon to predict with certainty that such an effect in Britain may also follow the Falklands conflict.

19

THE EMPIRE STRIKES BACK

The order to Rear Admiral Woodward to put his men ashore
followed swiftly at the end of the diplomatic negotiations. He
had a formidable force at his command, his warships, supported by forty-six merchant vessels, carried some 5,000
fighting men commanded by Brigadier Julian Thompson,
Commander of Three Commando Brigade. This Brigade
consisted of a headquarters and three Commandos, No 40,
No 42 and No 45. The Brigade also contained Royal Artillery, Royal Engineer and logistic units. With them were the
2nd and 3rd Battalions of the Parachute Regiment, two
troops of the Blues and Royals with their lightweight Scim-
itar and Scorpion tanks, air defence units with Rapier anti-
aircraft missile batteries and other units of supporting arms.
Behind this first wave, which was carried on the assault ships
Fearless and *Intrepid*, various warships, the ferry *Norland* and
the liner *Canberra*, came the *Queen Elizabeth II* with the three
thousand men of 5 Infantry Brigade commanded by Brigadier Tony Wilson. Its major components were the 2nd
Battalion, The Scots Guards, commanded by Lieutenant
Colonel Michael Scott, 1st Battalion, The Welsh Guards,
commanded by Lieutenant Colonel John Rickett and 1/7
Gurkha Rifles, commanded by Lieutenant Colonel D. P. de
C. Morgan. Also embarked on the *QEII* were support units
such as the 9th Parachute Squadron, Royal Engineers. For
the crew of the *Canberra*, the order for the invasion to start
came as something of a relief, for at times it seemed as if the
men of the Parachute Regiment and the Royal Marines
would just as soon fight each other as the Argentines when
unit rivalry and boredom combined to fray tempers.

Facing them were the 7–10,000 men landed by the Argentines, concentrated mainly around Stanley but with considerable garrisons at Darwin and Goose Green airstrip and at Fox Bay on West Falkland. They had mobile artillery armoured vehicles and some French AMX 13 tanks. All conscripts, except for some Marine commando units, they were not thought to be a match man for man with the professional British soldiers who had been battle-hardened in Northern Ireland. But in a reversal of military teaching (which recommends that the attacker outnumber the defender three to one), they considerably outnumbered the British. This advantage, however, was dissipated by the Argentines need to garrison a number of points on the island.

The Argentines retained throughout the conflict the great advantage of having a large fleet of aircraft based at airfields on the mainland which were untouchable. The Argentine Air Force had lost a number of aircraft, but it retained its numerical superiority over the British task force, although the Harriers too had been reinforced and some forty Sea Harriers and RAF ground assault Harriers were now flying from the carriers.

Brigadier General Lami Dozo had about 175 combat aircraft, the most dangerous to the fleet being the Super Etendards with their Exocet missiles. It was believed that there were six of these aircraft, but they would not be wasted over the battlefield. Their prime targets were the aircraft carriers. The task of combatting the Harriers would be given to the forty-two Mirage and Dagger interceptors which could also carry bombs and rockets. Then there were nine ageing British-built Canberra bombers which could hardly be risked over the battlefield in daylight. The main burden of the Argentine aerial attack was carried by their seventy-nine remaining A4 Skyhawk bombers, tough little planes which proved themselves in Vietnam and the Middle East. They carry a bomb-load of 4,000 lbs, and can fly close to the speed of sound defending themselves with cannon and air-to-air rockets. Then there were the thirty-nine remaining

Pucaras which fly at only 260 mph but are heavily armoured
and are designed to operate against ground forces. They are
armed with two 30mm cannon, four machine guns and
nearly 4,000 lbs of bombs and rockets. It was believed that
despite the SAS raid some of them were still flying from grass
airstrips on the Falklands. The problem for the aircraft based
on the mainland was that they were forced to operate at
extreme range giving them only a few minutes over the
battlefield.

Given that the Argentines' only real advantage was in the
air, it was obvious that in any major landing the destroyers
and frigates of the task force would have to expose themselves
to attack in order to protect the landing forces with their
anti-aircraft missiles, at least until the soldiers were able to
set up their own Rapier missile batteries ashore. It was not
possible initially for the Harriers to guarantee protection
from waves of enemy planes.

To offset the dangers to the fleet of air attack unorthodox
methods of trying to destroy aircraft such as the Super
Etendard on the ground had to be considered. Such operations were shrouded in secrecy. What is known for certain is
that a Sea King helicopter crashed in Chile far from the fleet
but near an Argentine air base. Chilean intelligence sources
were later quoted as the source of information that five
British 'commandos' had penetrated Rio Grande airfield to
destroy five Etendards.

Still worried by the air threat Admiral Woodward went
ahead to launch one of the most extraordinary operations ever
conceived by a British commander.

Friday, 21 May

The *Fearless*, and, incredibly, the great white luxury liner, the
Canberra, steamed into the dangerous waters of Falkland
Sound in the clear cold night of Thursday, 20 May, their
protecting frigates and destroyers screening them from

attack while anti-submarine helicopters busied themselves around the ships, probing the coves and inlets for the two Argentine submarines known to be at large. On the other side of East Falkland Island the carriers, *Hermes* and *Invincible*, took up station ready to launch their Harriers. Decoy attacks went in at Darwin, Goose Green and Fox Bay. Frigates shelled Stanley. It must have seemed a normal busy night to the Argentine garrison. But as the rumble of naval gunfire and the thud of 1,000 lb bombs echoed over the peat-bogs, and star shells hung eerily in the sky, the troopships moved closer inshore, unseen and unheard, while the frigates formed their defensive screen in the Sound. Ashore, patrols of the SBS and SAS waited to guide the landing force from the beaches. The Paras and the Marines gathered in their units on deck, their faces blacked, laden with equipment and weapons, writing last letters, drinking mugs of cocoa, some of them skylarking, burning off the nervous tension of waiting. Every one of them adjusting to the knowledge that shortly, very shortly, they were going into battle.

Port San Carlos was their objective. It had a good anchorage, was sheltered by hills from wind and low flying planes and, until a few days previously, had seen little of the Argentine Army.

At four a.m. the Marine Commandos and the Para-troopers began clambering down nets slung over the side of the ships to take their places in the landing craft. It was that pre-dawn time which always seems the darkest. The only light came from the electric wands of the loading officers as they brought the landing craft alongside and the faint flutter of white from the ensigns on the sterns of the landing craft. It was strangely quiet too, except for the distant gunfire and the muffled roar of the small boats' engines.

The men went ashore, unopposed, down the ramps, into the shallow water and up on to the beach, as in a Second World War film. Then firing broke out from Fanning Head, the point overlooking the invasion beaches which had been occupied by Argentine soldiers only a few days before.

Signals flickered from the hillside; 4.5 shells thumped into the Argentine positions. There was a crackle of small arms fire. Then silence. The garrison, numbering about two hundred, had fled, leaving some wounded and nine prisoners in British hands. They were to have some sort of revenge, because later, as they moved towards Stanley, they shot down two army Gazelle helicopters with hand-held rockets.

The disembarkation seemed to go on agonisingly slowly as the men queued to get into the landing craft. Some of the craft broke down and drifted in the bay and other small ships moved among them to nudge them to safety.

Then the news came that the beaches had been secured. The tanks of the Blues and Royals rolled ashore. The first of the heavy equipment was unloaded as the soldiers moved inland, setting up the defensive perimeter for the battle which they were sure had to come. They were welcomed with mugs of tea by Falklanders at the San Carlos settlement. As one of the islanders put it: "We were getting fed up with waiting for you. Every morning we've been saying, 'perhaps it'll be today, perhaps tomorrow'."

As dawn broke, men on the ships could see an astonishing sight: the anchorage crowded with ships and with landing craft buzzing backwards and forwards carrying load after load of men who disappeared inland until the hills seemed to be crawling with them. Vehicles criss-crossed the beach, directed by naval beachmasters. Helicopters, their guns and equipment slung beneath them, swung off the ships. It was a stirring sight but one that would surely have given the directors of the P&O line heart failure to see their beautiful *Canberra*, all £16 million of her, in the thick of the affair. Their concern would have been justified for with the dawn came the inevitability of attack from the air.

To the Argentine observers the fleet must have seemed an incredible sight, both because of its size and the power it represented and the sheer richness of the targets available to their Air Force – there was no question of the fleet coming out to do battle, it was bottled up in Argentine waters by Britain's nuclear submarines. But there was *Canberra, Fear-*

less, *Intrepid*, and an armada of landing ships, and to defend them there were only forty Harriers at the most and the screen of missile firing frigates and destroyers which had already shown themselves vulnerable to air attack. It was the target for which General Dozo had been saving his planes and pilots and now, before the beach-head had been firmly established with the heavy equipment ashore and Rapier missile batteries set up, the invasion fleet was at its most vulnerable. The big ships had to stay at anchor in the bay in order to complete the landing and the warship screen had to be maintained in the Sound to protect them. For the Argentine pilots it would not be a question of where the target is, but which target shall I go for?

The Harriers patrolled between the fleet and the Argentine mainland. But the first attack came from a Pucara flying from one of the Falklands' grass airstrips. It appeared suddenly, hugging the contours of the hill above the bay. It loosed off its rockets at a frigate, missed, and then disappeared back over the hill, followed by anti-aircraft fire sparkling with tracers and the glowing tails of rockets. That was the start of a long and bloody day, which may have been far removed by technology and distance from the 1940 Stuka raids on shipping at Dover's Hellfire Corner, but which was very close in the basic realities of air–sea warfare. The real danger showed when the mainland woke up to the significance of the invasion. Brian Hanrahan of the BBC saw the Argentine counter-attack start: "Two Mirages came sweeping down across the bay. We didn't see them at first. We saw the red wake of the anti-aircraft missiles rushing out to meet them. Then there was the roar of their engines, the explosion of bombs, missiles, guns – everybody firing together.

"One stray missile went off in the air about a hundred yards away. Two bombs exploded harmlessly on the hilltops as the planes curved away. And then the planes came pouring in, wave after wave of them." Hanrahan admitted: "I was just too confused to keep track of what was going on. As the day went on, more of the attacks came from the Skyhawk fighter-bombers. In one short period ten or a dozen

Skyhawk bombers dived down on the ships at anchor, producing the same barrage of fire and counter-fire."

Other reports spoke of British missiles actually dog-fighting with Argentine missiles, with the attacking missiles attempting to evade those fired at them from the T22 frigates in the defensive screen. The big ships were protected to some extent by the hills surrounding the bay but the frigates out in the Sound, who had to remain on station, had no such protection. The Mirages and the Skyhawks had a clear run at them. The most exposed was *Ardent*, the five-year-old Type 21 based at Plymouth and armed with Exocet surface-to-surface missiles and Seacat anti-aircraft missiles. She was bombarding Goose Green when a flight of five Mirages attacked her. Sea Harriers shot down two of the Mirages but they riddled *Ardent* with rockets. Dead in the water, her aluminium super-structure burning, she had to be abandoned and sank with twenty-two dead. Another frigate was hit by a 1,000 lb bomb in the engine room. If it had exploded it would have destroyed the ship but it did not, and although it put the engines out of action, its guns and missiles continued to fire. Three other ships were hit and two sailors killed but the ships were not seriously damaged. Miraculously, it seemed, the big landing ships came through it all unscathed, although the Argentine pilots pressed home their attacks with courage and skill. Some of them used the lob technique of pulling their planes up as they approached their targets thus throwing their bombs forward, while they were able to manoeuvre away from the anti-aircraft fire.

Meanwhile the troops ashore were having their own problems with the Pucaras. Their platoon officers blew whistles and ordered them to keep down when these soldier-killers came creeping over the hills. The troops fired back with machine-guns and their hand-held Blowpipe missiles and thanked the SAS for having taken out six of the Argentines' Pucaras in their raid on Pebble Island.

In one of the tragedies of this conflict, nineteen members of the SAS along with a Marine corporal and an RAF Flight Lieutenant were lost in a helicopter accident as they were taking off for yet another raid in support of the landings. Their names will be inscribed on the memorial clock tower at their headquarters in Hereford. They did not, in SAS parlance, "beat the clock".

The soldiers, as they dug in on the hillsides, could not see the toll being taken of the Argentine aircraft, particularly the Mirages, by the Harriers patrolling between the Falklands and the Argentine coast. They and their pilots performed brilliantly. The plane, which had been written off because it was argued by many that it could not carry enough fuel and weapons, proved itself beyond doubt this day, shooting down eight Argentine aircraft. It is salutary to note that without those forty Harriers it would have been impossible to mount the expedition at all. Just one Harrier was lost in this day's fighting, while nine Mirages, five Skyhawks and two Pucaras were shot down by the Harriers and the fleet's anti-aircraft fire. Four Argentine helicopters were also destroyed.

The aerial fighting went on all day, the sky clamorous with planes and shells and rockets. Exploding aircraft cartwheeled across the sky and a great column of smoke rose from the dying *Ardent*. Only darkness brought an end to the fighting.

It had been an historic day. The Argentines had inflicted a cruel blow on the fleet by sinking *Ardent* and it was only by the grace of God, a faulty fuse, and the bravery of the Harrier pilots and the anti-aircraft ships, that the losses had not been more. The Super Etendards and their feared Exocets had taken no part in the battle, although just about everything else had been thrown at the task force. But the Argentines had suffered a very bloody nose, losing some of their best pilots and taking losses which were estimated at nearly half of the attacking aircraft. A great number had been badly damaged and it was thought unlikely that they would get back to the mainland – and that meant the loss not only of the aircraft but also of the pilot.

When the clamour died away, the British had landed some 5,000 men and occupied ten square miles, while sending strong raiding parties into other areas of both main islands.

They had tanks ashore and, most important of all, Rapier anti-aircraft missile batteries, to protect the troops and to cover the ships still unloading in the bay. Earth-moving equipment had been landed and work started on assembling prefabricated take-off pads for Harriers. Meanwhile, unlike their pilots, the Argentine Army did nothing to repel the attackers, but sat in their positions around Stanley and waited to be attacked.

On the mainland the newspapers screamed "Victory" and printed extravagant claims of ships sunk and Harriers shot down while, they said, the few British forces which had managed to get ashore were in hiding and surrounded, waiting "for a Dunkirk".

The reality was that a sizeable force of professional British soldiers had established a considerable footing on the islands and equipment was pouring ashore. The Union Jack had been raised once again on the Falkland Islands.

Saturday, 22 May

The unloading of supplies and the licking of wounds continued throughout the night. British and Argentine wounded were treated side by side in the *Canberra*. The troops ashore consolidated their positions, preparing a springboard for their attack inland. Harriers patrolled the skies, shooting up an Argentine vessel, and the frigates bombarded Argentine positions. At the United Nations, the Security Council debate continued in a welter of Latin American passion while in London, Admiral Sir Terence Lewin, Chief of Defence Staff said, "We are going to move fast. You can expect a great deal of activity within the next few days."

·But there was no sign at all of the Argentine Air Force. The pilots, who had been so determined the day before, were missing from the skies and their absence gave the landing force something they had prayed for but never expected, a whole day free of attack from the air. By the end of the day the British land forces were no longer vulnerable.

Sunday, 23 May

The Argentine Air Force returned to the fight with determination despite its losses. Fierce air and missile-to-missile battles raged over Falkland Sound and the beaches, where supplies continued to be ferried ashore by landing craft and pontoons. Rapier missile batteries, now ashore, joined in the battle as Skyhawks and Mirages swept over the anchorage through a curtain of fire, with anti-aircraft missiles chasing after the planes and bombs dropped between the ships. HMS *Antelope*, sister ship of the *Ardent*, was hit by a Skyhawk which was itself destroyed seconds after it dropped its bombs. One 500 lb bomb lodged in the engine room but did not explode. An explosives officer set to work to defuse it but it exploded as he worked on it. He was killed and fierce fires raced through the ship. The crew fought all day to save their ship but in the end were forced to abandon her, a burning hulk in the Falkland Sound. But the Argentines paid dearly for their success. They lost five Mirages and one Skyhawk. A further Mirage and a Skyhawk were thought to have been brought down. Harriers also destroyed two helicopters and damaged another. The casualty list for the task force since it set sail was seventy-one dead. The Security Council continued to talk: the Panamanian delegate abused Mrs Thatcher and Mrs Jeane Kirkpatrick, the US delegate, said his attacks were sexist. Meanwhile, the beach-head continued to expand as more materiel poured ashore and the Marines and Paratroopers started probing along the road to Stanley.

Monday, 24 May

The Mirages and the Skyhawks returned to the attack and damaged two British supply ships, but six Mirages and two

Skyhawks were shot down and others were damaged. Questions began to be asked about the morale of the Argentine pilots. Despite many empty places at the Mess table, they continued to press their attacks with determination. To supplement the Harriers and missiles, machine-guns manned by Royal Marines were set up on ships' decks to fire directly upward, making a screen through which straffing aircraft would have to fly. Blowpipe missiles, hand-held anti-aircraft missiles fired by one man, joined in the fight. The bridgehead began to disappear into the hills as helicopters shuttled the heavy equipment off the beach. A field hospital was set up ashore. Ships, including the *Canberra*, moved out of the bay to safety after they had delivered their loads. The SAS, the SBS and frigates harassed Argentine positions with gunfire. There is speculation that the SAS had carried out a raid on the Rio Gallegos base in southernmost Argentina in order to knock out the Super Etendards. A British Harrier crashed on take-off and its pilot was killed. The *Queen Elizabeth II* arrived with her 3,500 troops. Back in London, Mr John Nott told the House of Commons "a very tough fight might be ahead", and that naval reinforcements had more than compensated for the task force's losses. However, disquiet was expressed about the use of aluminium – a fire hazard – in Britain's frigates. In Washington, Ireland formally submitted a resolution to the UN Security Council calling for a seventy-two-hour ceasefire which would allow the renewal of the Security Council's peace initiative.

The EEC voted to continue sanctions against Argentina for an indefinite period. Italy and Ireland opted out but agreed not to break the sanctions.

Tuesday, 25 May

This was Argentina's National Day, and the task force prepared for the attack they felt was sure to come. When it came it was concentrated on HMS *Coventry*, which was on

radar picket duty with HMS *Broadsword*, off the northern
entrance of Falkland Sound. At first the battle went Britain's
way. The *Coventry* shot down a reconnaissance aircraft with a
Sea Dart missile and then knocked down all four Skyhawks
which came in to attack her. But later in the afternoon the
fortunes of war changed dramatically. Four more Skyhawks
caught *Coventry* by surprise, flying low over Pebble Island to
penetrate the radar defences, and hit her with bombs. *Broadsword* was also slightly damaged but picked up the *Coventry*'s
crew when the stricken ship capsized. Twenty-one men died
in her. Worse was to follow an hour later when the 14,946 ton
Atlantic Conveyor, requisitioned from Cunard, was making her
way round the north-east tip of the Falklands to enter the
Sound with a cargo which included helicopters, spares for the
Harriers and hundreds of tons of equipment for the land
forces. Two Super Etendard aircraft fired Exocet missiles at
her. One missed but the other hit hard. She caught fire and
had to be abandoned. Twelve of her crew, including her
master, Captain Ian North, were lost.

It was Britain's worst day of the conflict so far. The
Coventry's loss was acceptable, although tragic, because she
was in the most exposed position of all, to give warning to the
beach-head and the ships unloading in the bay. As Mr Nott
pointed out, another ten frigates and destroyers had arrived
to more than replace the naval losses. But the *Atlantic Conveyor*
sinking was more serious. The loss of the supplies she was
carrying could possibly hold up the break-out from the
beach-head which now seemed imminent. And she would
cost £20 million to replace. These losses dispelled the previous day's euphoria, brought about by the toll taken of
Argentine planes. However, there was some consolation
derived from the fact that the Argentines had used two of
their precious Exocets on the container ship. It was thought
possible that her size and shape had convinced the Argentine
pilots, firing by radar, that she was one of the aircraft
carriers, whose loss would have been disastrous. The Argentines were scouring the world's arms markets to rebuild their
stock of Exocets. It was now believed that they had used five,

three having been expended in the *Sheffield* attack, in which the carrier *Invincible* was the main target. This meant that they could be down to a single missile. Reports came through that contact had been made with small parties of Argentine soldiers in the Goose Green area which was being probed by British special forces.

The Irish withdrew their resolution at the United Nations. It was announced that Captain Astiz was being brought back to England by sea as he was still wanted by Sweden and France for questioning about the fate of a Swedish girl and two French nuns who had "disappeared".

Wednesday, 26 May

After their success of the previous day, the Argentine Air Force stayed at home while Harriers raided Stanley airport. The feeling was growing that British troops were ready to launch an attack, in an attempt to end the conflict swiftly. The United Nations Security Council unanimously approved a watered-down resolution, asking the Secretary General to try to arrange a cease-fire, while in London criticism mounted about the way in which the Defence Ministry was handling the news of the loss of ships. The long delay between the announcement that a ship had been hit and the release of her name and number of casualties was proving very hard on the families of the men with the task force, indicating how poorly the Ministry's handling of news compared with the success of its other duties in the crisis.

Thursday, 27 May

This was the day of the break-out. Rear Admiral Woodward's gamble had succeeded for, although the Task Force's losses had been severe, it had accomplished its task of getting the troops and their equipment ashore. It had been an astonishing episode in British naval history in which just about every hard-learned lesson of the dangers of operating off a hostile shore without air supremacy had been ignored – not out of choice, but because Rear Admiral Woodward had no other alternative. Despite the Argentine pilots' bravery, one captured pilot reported that half his squadron had been shot down in operations over the islands. The Harriers, the missile barrier and the wall of machine gun fire had enabled the task force commander to carry out his mission. The sailors had shown great skill and courage and the men who moved the equipment ashore, the unsung heroes of the Royal Corps of Transport, had performed valiantly, carrying on with the task of unloading fuel and ammunition by motorised rafts even though they were soaked with water thrown up by near-misses.

There followed rumours of an assault. And Mrs Thatcher told an expectant House of Commons that the troops were moving out of the bridgehead. She would not give details but it later became known that one company of the 2nd Battalion of the Parachute Regiment had moved south east towards Darwin into the area of Camilla Creek House on Wednesday night. This was in order to secure a start line for an assault by the rest of the Battalion on the Argentine positions at Darwin and Goose Green. They had fought a sharp action with an Argentine patrol and captured four men. Throughout daylight on Thursday the rest of the heavily laden Battalion moved forward over the rough terrain but waited until nightfall to take up their assault positions. A Royal Artillery troop of 105mm light guns and the Paras' own 81mm mortars were flown in by helicopter to provide direct fire support.

At the same time Royal Marine Commandos and the 3rd Battalion of the Parachute Regiment moved out along the Northern route to Stanley. Frigates and the Harriers continued their harrassing attacks on the Argentine positions while for the first time Argentinian Skyhawks turned their attention from the ships to the men and stores in the bridgehead. It was as if they knew that they had failed to stop the landing and had to switch their attacks to the Army. Six Marines and a Royal Engineer were killed when two pairs of

Skyhawks made a low level run over the trenches. Two of the
Skyhawks were shot down. The Argentines later claimed
that their Canberra bombers had been in action, mounting a
night raid over the British positions.

It was discovered that the *Atlantic Conveyor* was still afloat
after the fires on board had burnt out, and she was reboarded
to see if she could be towed to safety or if any of her cargo
could be saved. The hospital ship *Uganda* entered Falkland
Sound to pick up British and Argentine wounded, amongst a
barrage of complaints from the junta that it was engaging in
military activity and was liable to be bombed. The three
crewmen of the Sea King helicopter which had landed and
been destroyed in Chile, returned to England telling an
unconvincing story that they had become lost while on
patrol. The United States announced it was supplying Britain with equipment – especially Sidewinder air-to-air missiles and perforated steel planking to construct landing pads
for Harriers.

Friday, 28 May

On this day the 2nd Battalion of the Parachute Regiment
under the command of Lieutenant Colonel Herbert Jones
fought one of the most skillful and courageous battles in the
history of the British Army. The Battalion set out at two
o'clock in the morning from its start line at Camilla Creek
House to take Darwin, the second largest settlement in the
Falklands, and Goose Green, the airstrip five miles to the
south. It was committed to a frontal attack over open ground
against a numerically superior enemy in prepared positions,
a situation which every soldier hates. But Lieutenant Colonel
Jones, known simply as "H" to all his men, had no option.
Darwin and Goose Green lie on the narrow neck of land
joining the two parts of East Falkland. There was no possibility of an outflanking attack because the Argentine positions
had the sea on either side of them. The Paras knew they had
to fight their way across the isthmus with only their two

105mm guns and mortars to support them. The frigates
which had bombarded the Argentine positions during the
night withdrew as dawn came and low cloud prevented the
Harriers from giving close support. They were on their own.

Darwin, the first objective, fell without too much trouble.
But as the Paras pressed on down the isthmus they met
stiffening resistance. They had to take each strongpoint but
as they moved forward, they came under fire from mortars
and machine-guns. The Paras became grateful for the peaty
soil which they had found such a burden to cross: it absorbed
the blast of the mortars and cut down the effect of the
shrapnel. The Argentines put up six of their Pucara straffing
planes to attack the British. They shot down a Scout helicopter but four of them were knocked out of the sky by
Blowpipe missiles and small-arms fire. According to Colonel
Christopher Dunphie of the Royal Marines who is chief of
staff to the Military Deputy to Commander in Chief, Fleet, it
was now that the battalion came up against the main Argentine defensive positions.

The Paras were well dug in and sited in depth. The
resistance became fierce and in particular two well-sited
heavy machine-guns kept the Paras pinned down for about
half an hour. It was in these circumstances that Lieutenant
Colonel Jones and his Adjutant, Captain David Wood themselves led a platoon attack on the machine-gun nests. "H"
always led from the front. He and his Adjutant were killed in
the assault but they had so inspired their men that the
machine-gun posts were wiped out. The attack, said Colonel
Dunphie, was carried out with the "utmost courage and
determination". There is always the danger that when an
officer as respected as "H" is killed the shock produces a
numbing effect on his men, but in this case the second in
command, Major Christopher Keeble, immediately took
over and urged his men on. Dunphie reported that the "hard
infantry slogging match was instantly resumed, in which the
brilliant qualities of the Parachute Regiment were splendidly
displayed."

It was the turning point of the battle. The cloud lifted and three Harriers scythed through the Argentine positions with anti-personnel cluster bombs and by dusk the Paras had the remaining Argentines bottled up in Goose Green settlement. The battle had now been in progress for fourteen hours. Argentine prisoners and British casualties were brought back as mortars thumped into the gorse bushes. Darkness fell and Major Keeble tried to bring an end to the fighting. Using the inter-settlement short wave radios of Mr Allan Miller, manager of Port Carlos settlement, and Mr Eric Goss, manager of Goose Green settlement, he negotiated with the Argentine commanders in Goose Green. The negotiations went on throughout the night until Air Commodore Wilson Drozier Podrozo, the Argentine Air Force commander and Lt Col Halo Piaggi, the military force commander, agreed to meet under "white flag conditions" at the edge of Goose Green airfield at 9 a.m. on Saturday.

Major Keeble made his way through to the Paras who, although weary after two nights without sleep and showing the strains of battle, were ready to attack the Argentine perimeter whenever he gave the word. But the Argentines had no more stomach for the fight. After agreeing to release the 114 civilians they had been holding under guard in the settlement's recreation centre for thirty days, they were willing to surrender. Air Commodore Podrozo paraded his men on the airstrip and delivered a political speech to them. They sang the Argentine National Anthem and laid down their weapons and helmets. It was an act of surrender befitting the Argentine character – full of style – but it was noticed that when one group laid down their rifles they cheered with relief. All they wanted to do was to go home, as far away as possible from the *Islas Malvinas*.

The Paras were astonished to discover that they had taken some 1400 prisoners. There is no doubt that the Argentine strength at Darwin and Goose Green had been far greater than the Paras had expected and although most of them were conscripts, nevertheless they had outnumbered the British by more than two to one with the added advantage of fighting from well-prepared positions. For one battalion of some 600

men to attack and defeat them was an epic feat of arms. Apart
from their prisoners, the Paras also captured large quantities
of arms and equipment, including three howitzers, four
anti-aircraft guns and three unserviceable Pucaras. At the
same time they rescued Squadron Leader Bob Iveson, who
had ejected from his crashing Harrier on Thursday and had
hidden, waiting until he knew that British troops were near
before showing himself. The Paras had lost fifteen dead and
thirty-one wounded. One Marine helicopter pilot and one
Royal Engineers Commando were also killed. (In 1979 the
2nd Battalion had lost eighteen men including a Lieutenant
Colonel in a Provisional IRA bomb ambush at Warren-
point.)

The taking of the two settlements was vital to the whole
progress of Rear Admiral Woodward's ultimate step, the
retaking of Stanley. By recapturing Darwin he had secured
his right flank and he had opened up the Southern route of a
pincer movement on Stanley, for while the Paras were taking
Darwin, the Royal Marines and the 3rd Battalion of the
Parachute Regiment had moved along the Northern Route
and taken the settlements of Douglas and Teal Inlet. They
met light opposition but it took them thirty-six hours to make
their way to Teal Inlet across the mud and peat bog.

Rear Admiral Woodward was also able to land the Guards
and Gurkhas who had been carried to the Falklands by the
Queen Elizabeth II. By taking Goose Green he had provided
the Harriers with a base only sixty miles from Stanley. He
had also delivered a severe blow to the prestige of the junta
and the morale of the Argentine Army. The Union flag and
the Parachute Regiment's Pegasus flew over Goose Green
and Darwin while the dead were carried away, the wounded
treated and the prisoners herded into makeshift compounds.

Saturday, 29 May

The officers and men who had died in Friday's fighting were
buried by the Paratroopers in one big grave behind the

medical aid post at San Carlos. The chaplain conducted the
service, the Regimental Sergeant Major threw a handful of
soil onto the coffins. But there was no ceremonial, no volleys
of rifle-fire, no mourning bugle.

There were many tributes to "H". Major Keeble insisted:
"The victory is entirely his. It was H's plan that worked."
Mrs Thatcher spoke of "this truly valiant and courageous
officer who was loved by his men." And his wife, Sara, told
reporters: "He died as he lived – a soldier. He wouldn't have
wanted it any other way. I know that as long as we win in the
end, it will have been worthwhile. That is the way he would
have felt."

At Darwin and Goose Green, stories of petty meanness by
the Argentine soldiers began to emerge. They had looted
houses, broken furniture, defecated on the floor and shot
around a shepherd from a helicopter as he was tending his
sheep. The Paras put some of their prisoners to work cleaning
up the mess while the bulk were transferred to prison compounds at Ajax Bay in the bridgehead area. The Ministry of
Defence announced that hospital ships were being brought in
to evacuate both British and Argentine wounded and it
seemed likely they would be taken to Montevideo for transfer
to hospitals. "Other Argentine prisoners," said the Ministry
of Defence, "will be transferred to the Royal Fleet Auxiliary
Sir Percival and a requisitioned merchant ship. This transfer
may take some time to complete due to the numbers and
distances involved. The ships will then take the prisoners out
of the operational area."

In Buenos Aires all that the junta would admit was that
radio contact with Goose Green had been lost. But officials
began to prepare the public for bad news with stories that the
garrisons at Darwin and Goose Green had not been reinforced and were heavily outnumbered by the British forces.
In a speech at Army Headquarters, celebrating the 172nd
anniversary of the founding of the Argentine Army, President Galtieri reaffirmed Argentina's commitment to the
battle but at the end of the speech he made some significant
comments: "To the millions of men and women from our

homeland and from other American countries who come to offer themselves as volunteers, thank you. I have no more weapons, nor cannons, nor tanks for them. We have no more ships or planes to be manned. May it be God's wish that when this unequal fight against the extra-continental aggressor and those who support him is over, the torch we have hoisted to illuminate the awakening of America and those who have been deprived in the world, may never go out."

In fact the only forces that now stood between the British and total victory were the now depleted Argentine Air Force and the 8,000 men dug in around Stanley. Much depended on their morale. They had been hammered from the air and the sea. They had been virtually cut off from supplies. They knew that the British Army was on the way. The weather was cold and miserable and they were hungry and far from home. The regular units of the Marines could be relied upon to give a good account of themselves. But what of the young conscripts? Would they run or stay and fight?

Meanwhile, the fighting continued. The Argentine air raids were fewer and were pressed with less determination than previously. One Skyhawk was shot down. The British consolidated their position at Darwin and began to push forward along the southern route to Stanley while in the north the mixed force of Paras and Commandos continued their advance towards the Argentine positions on the high ground protecting the town. The stage was being set for the next act in Rear Admiral Woodward's carefully planned drama. Since his unfortunate experiences with reporters early in the conflict he had not said a single word for publication. Neither triumph nor tragedy has moved him to speak. He had allowed his actions to speak for him.

Sunday, 30 May

The task force mounted its heaviest bombardment of Stanley, and Harriers joined in the pounding of Argentine positions, softening them up while the ground forces made their way closer and closer to the Argentine perimeter. There was still no news of the Guards and Gurkhas, the trump card that the task force commander was playing very close to his chest. But it became known that Major General Jeremy Moore, the Marine who always goes into battle with a Bible in his breast pocket, had arrived to take command of all the land forces. The Argentime Air Force returned to its attacks on the fleet, trying to knock out one of the carriers with Skyhawks using bombs and Super Etendards with their deadly Exocets, and Buenos Aires claimed that *Invincible* was badly damaged. In Whitehall it was estimated that the Argentines' supply of Exocets was getting low. They had only scored two hits with these missiles, the rest having missed. One of their problems was that the Super Etendard is not a particularly good air-craft and it carries only one Exocet under the starboard wing, which must be balanced by a fuel tank under the port. If the pilot is not expert the aircraft becomes unstable at the moment of release. It seemed that these later attacks were very much last ditch affairs and Michael Nicholson of ITN reported that in one attack a C130 transport plane was used as a bomber with bombs being rolled out of the rear doors. Whatever else may be said about the Argentines, their Air Force never lacked guts.

Meanwhile private quarrels broke out among the politicians. In Buenos Aires the junta was said to be quarrelling fiercely over who was to blame for the defeat which they now assumed was inevitable. In London it was reported that relations had become badly strained between Mrs Thatcher and Mr Pym. It was said that Mr Pym's line – and the consistent line of the Foreign Office – was that whatever the outcome of the fighting, negotiations would eventually have to take place with the junta, or whoever was ruling Argentina. But Mrs Thatcher was insisting that those days were over and that she was thinking in terms of the future development of the Falklands as British territory.

In Washington, the US news magazine *Newsweek* printed an account of a bitter dispute between Secretary of State Alexander Haig and Mrs Jeane Kirkpatrick, the US representative at the United Nations. According to the magazine, the quarrel erupted in a heated forty-five minute telephone conversation in which Mrs Kirkpatrick accused Mr Haig of being too pro-British and he accused her of being too pro-Argentine. Mr Haig was quoted as saying that Mrs Kirkpatrick is "mentally and emotionally incapable of thinking clearly on this issue because of her close links with the Latins", while Mrs Kirkpatrick was said to have accused the Secretary of State and his aides of being "amateurs . . . totally insensitive to Latin cultures". She was also scornful of Mr Haig's support of Britain, describing it as a "boy's club vision of gang loyalty".

Meanwhile the Pope, on his pastoral visit to Britain, continued to call for peace. War, he said, was "totally unacceptable as a means of settling differences between nations."

Monday, 31 May

The build-up for the assault on Stanley continued with British troops seizing Mount Kent, a key observation post ten miles to the west of the Falklands capital. It was regarded as the gateway to Stanley and from its 1,500 ft summit virtually every Argentine position could be observed and shelled by 105mm guns carried into position by Chinook helicopters. First reports indicated that casualties in the fighting were light and that no British troops were killed. It was believed that General Menendez had pulled most of his soldiers back into the Stanley perimeter in order to concentrate his fighting men. The odds, previously in favour of the Argentines, had changed dramatically with the fall of Goose Green and Darwin. With other garrisons left "to wither on the vine" on West Falkland and the southern half of East Falkland, it was estimated that General Menendez possibly had as few as 6,000 men to defend Stanley and even this total included significant numbers of airmen and sailors who were not trained to fight against professional British Marines and

Paras. The battle for Goose Green made it clear that this was a greater victory for the British than was at first realised. The Argentines suffered 250 dead. The Paras also discovered some 9,000 gallons of Napalm which the Argentines had been mixing for their Pucaras to drop. Mrs Linda Dixon, whose eighteen-year-old son Stephen had been killed alongside Lieutenant Colonel H. Jones, said that she had been told how they died by a Parachute Regiment officer. "He said the battalion was pinned down by machine-gun fire and mortar bombardment from two sides. They could not move either way and the CO called for volunteers to storm the machine-gun positions with him. They all knew it could be suicidal but my son stepped forward and he was one of the seventeen chosen to go with Colonel 'H'."

A number of lessons were learned by the British. The first was that the Argentines, even though most of them were young conscripts, could fight well from prepared positions. The second was that although they were hungry they were plentifully supplied with arms and ammunition. The third was that the attack had been anticipated and preparations made to receive it. General Menendez had helicoptered in a battalion of regular Marines the day before the attack – a move which could cost him dear in the long run. Robert Fox of the BBC later reported that the whole of the Argentine strategic reserve had been committed to this battle.

Tuesday, 1 June

There was sporadic contact during the day as British forces probed at the Argentine perimeter and more and more soldiers slogged their way across the peat-bogs in driving sleet and rain with the temperature hovering around freezing. They were travelling light while the helicopters brought

up the heavy equipment ready for the final battle. One patrol
had a brisk firefight with a group of Argentines who had been
dropped by parachute near Teal Island four days previously
and had set up a strongpoint at a deserted house called Top
Malo House. They were members of the Argentine version of
the Special Air Service, Unit 602, some of whose members
had been trained by the British SAS. Well equipped and
armed, they put up stiff resistance when the British patrol
attacked them. The British fired anti-tank rockets into the
house, blew off the roof and set it on fire. The Argentines
came out fighting. Four were killed and seven wounded
before they surrendered. Three of the British patrol were
wounded.

General Menendez, preparing for the British assault,
called on his men "to inflict a crushing defeat. The eyes of the
nation are on you and you must not let the people down."

Wednesday, 2 June

The build-up to the battle for Stanley continued. Land
Rovers, tracked vehicles, helicopters and farm tractors carried supplies, ammunition and men up to the British positions on the high ground encircling the Argentine perimeter.
The *Sunday Telegraph* reporter, Charles Laurence, who was
attached to the Commandos, wrote of their "epic march"
from San Carlos to the capital: "Yomping, they call it in the
Royal Marine Commandos. It means marching, humping
up to 220 lbs of equipment and all the arms needed for attack
at the far end of the trek . . . the Falklands campaign has
turned the Commandos into a fearsome-looking troop. After
twelve days in the open, with camouflage cream on their
faces, they are wild, dirty and unshaven. Their clothes are
mud-stained and the dirt is ingrained into their hands. After
another day's march is done, even the most senior officers
look like hedge-stained tramps, but armed to the teeth and
ready to scare even the Vikings into a hasty retreat."

Men of the SAS took out Argentine positions on the twin peaks of the Two Sisters above Stanley and they were occupied without any British casualties. With binoculars the British could now see the Argentine soldiers eating their lunch in Stanley. Royal Artillery commando gunners began their bombardment from the newly captured ground, sending 105mm shells into Moody Brook, the former Royal Marine barracks which had been taken over by the Argentines as a Headquarters. Two Harriers were forced to ditch after being hit by ground fire, but both pilots were saved by helicopters. Everywhere there was the feeling of inevitability, that the final battle was only hours away. In Buenos Aires there was apprehension as the true situation seeped through the nationalistic fervour of the propaganda, whilst in London Mrs Thatcher made it plain that President Galtieri must withdraw his troops. She denied that she was seeking to humiliate the Argentines: "I am asking the invader to return his troops to the mainland. That is not humiliation. I am just trying to repossess islands which are British sovereign territory. That is liberty, justice and democracy." But when asked about the possibility of showing magnanimity towards Argentina, she replied: "Magnanimity is not a word I use in connection with the battle on the Falklands. To give that to an invader and aggressor and fascist dictators would be treason or a betrayal of our own people."

Thursday, 3 June

The British added psychological pressure to the bombardments and probing actions designed to undermine the morale of the Argentine garrison. Harriers scattered leaflets over the troops who had retreated into the Stanley perimeter. One side of the leaflets carried an open letter to General Menendez calling on him to surrender and the other was a safe conduct pass. The Argentine soldiers were promised

food and medical equipment and were told to "lay down your
weapons. Hold the pass in a prominent position. Move
forward to the nearest member of the British forces." An
RAF Vulcan was forced to land in Brazil after it missed its
rendezvous with a tanker aircraft and ran out of fuel. At the
United Nations Panama and Spain tried to cobble together a
compromise resolution to bring about a ceasefire.

Friday, 4 June

Fog enshrouded the battlefield almost as thickly as the news
blackout on the military preparations for the assault on
Stanley. In Paris Mrs Thatcher and President Reagan talked
for ninety minutes mainly about the Falklands. The indications were that the President tried to persuade Mrs Thatcher
to bring about a pause but Mr Haig, the American Secretary
of State, later denied that the United States had exerted any
such pressure. "There is no basis for this," he said. "It is not
in the United States lexicon to suggest such a pause. We
would not suggest it. And we do not presume to."

At the United Nations the joint Panamanian–Spanish
resolution was vetoed by Britain. Sir Anthony Parsons explained that the resolution was totally unacceptable to Britain because "there is no direct and inseparable link between
the ceasefire and immediate Argentine withdrawal in a fixed
time limit." Nine members voted for the resolution. Four
abstained, and the United States voted with Britain. As if to
highlight the ambivalence of the United States throughout
the crisis, Mrs Jeane Kirkpatrick, having said that the
United States vote affirmed "the principle that force should
not be allowed to triumph", then announced that her Government had really wished her to abstain. Mr Haig's decision
to abstain – taken without consulting President Reagan –
had not reached her in time. If it were possible to change her
country's vote, she said, she would do so. However, despite

the dithering by the United States, Britain's veto meant that the way was now open for Britain to retake Stanley by force of arms.

Saturday, 5 June

General Mario Menendez had surprised the British by the speed with which he pulled back almost all his forces within the Stanley perimeter after the battle at Goose Green. For the defence of the capital, he had assembled five or six battalions including 1,000 commandos. With the airmen and sailors who were also ashore, this gave him a force estimated to be around 7,000 strong, most of whom took up position outside the town.

The decision of General Menendez to race his troops into this position gave his opponents some clue to his military mentality. He was clearly not eager to fight out in open and difficult country, but preferred to allow himself to be hemmed in at the tip of the island with his back to the sea. It was a sign that he had acquired a siege mentality, and had thereby lost the capability for offensive action. Faced with the ultimate decision to fight or to surrender and withdraw, there were signs that he might be willing to fight only as long as military honour demanded.

The British began thinking there might be a possibility of reviving the old custom of civilised warfare, by which a beleaguered garrison might be accorded the honours of war and allowed to march out with their arms and with their flags flying before signing a document of surrender.

Meanwhile, although the fog and bad weather had stilled the fighting, preparations for the British assault on the garrison continued. Major General Jeremy Moore, who had taken over command, was determined to take no risks when his troops went in. He was no doubt conscious of the fact that

in the successful battle of Goose Green, the attacking battalion had been surprised by the strength of the Argentine
garrison. Military intelligence seems not to have been aware
that the Argentines had brought in 700 reserve fighting
troops by tractor drawn vehicles and helicopter. In the end
this benefitted the British because all the defenders were put
out of action by the surrender, but the episode was a warning
that caution was still necessary. He visited the advanced
positions, spoke of General Menendez being squeezed into a
little corner of the island and warned him: "He will be even
more squeezed before we are finished." Nonetheless the
British land force commander said that he did not want to go
dashing in, and thereby cause unnecessary casualties, but he
added that his troops were also prepared to receive any
counter-attack. British helicopters were whirling in with
artillery guns and with ammunition swinging through the
mist beneath them. So many were in position by Saturday
night that war correspondents with the troops were predict-
ing that the assault, when and if it came, would be preceded
by the biggest barrage of artillery shells fired since the end of
the Second World War. Nobody on the spot believed in
anything but a British victory which would force the Argentines from the islands.

It was known that the Argentine garrison in Stanley had
artillery pieces of 105mm and of 155mm calibre, as well as
81mm mortars, all protected by anti-aircraft guns. They
were also equipped with anti-tank and other missiles as well
as the British-made Blowpipe anti-aircraft missiles.

As the rival forces squared up for the fight it seemed as
though the state of affairs in the whole Falklands conflict had
come full circle from the time in April when the Argentines
took over Stanley. Now it was the turn of the Argentines to be
improvising defences, though their forces were a great deal
larger than those of the original British handful of defenders.
Just as the British had tried to boost morale by hinting at the
presence of submarines, the Argentines were now using black
propaganda to suggest that somehow they had managed to
get 2,000 troop reinforcements into the besieged capital. To

British troops watching the town through field glasses, this seemed a ludicrous claim.

Now it was the junta in Buenos Aires which began to display the signs of alarm and confusion which had originally been felt in London when the Falkland Islands were first seized. Although it did not appear that the Argentine government was in danger of being overthrown, President Galtieri was busy consulting with trade union chiefs and leaders of the old political parties, promising all manner of political and economic concessions in an effort to gain support. Although the population remained loyal, signs were beginning to appear of a general awareness that things were not going as well as they had been led to expect. "No one knows what is going to happen, only that the country is going to go through some profound conflicts," said Mario Campora, a former leader of the Peronist political party.

The Argentine Army and Air Force were frantically trying to re-stock their forces with "magic" weapons, the Exocets and the Gabriel ship-to-ship missiles, to strike back at the Royal Navy task force. They combed the world market of the arms trade, and made demands upon the armouries of friendly and neutral nations to acquire such missiles with the same determination that Hitler had put into getting his final "secret weapons" to snatch victory from defeat. There were indications too that the Air Force was managing to get extra fighting aircraft: Mirages and the Israeli-made Daggers.

In all the countries likely to provide such military help, British diplomats were ordered to do everything possible to discourage them from selling. Far away from the Falklands front, the British Secret Intelligence Service was involved in covert action to locate available stocks on the market, and to do everything possible to prevent them from passing into Argentine hands. The threat of final, desperate attempts to upset the balance of military power on the islands was taken very seriously.

Within the junta, arguments began between members of the triumvirate and of their supporting officers about what should be done. None of them wanted to give up the islands without a fight. But they were asking the same question which British Members of Parliament had begun asking much earlier: how much bloodshed were the islands worth? Now it was: how much Argentine blood? Not all the military officers were convinced that there was a great deal of point in trying to continue the war after the fall of Stanley by mounting air and submarine attacks. It might still be possible to get more from negotiation in the long run than by salvaging military honour at a very high price.

It was sixty-five days since the Argentine troops seized the islands. It was also the eve of an historic British military anniversary – D-Day.

CONCLUSION

The end of the beginning of the battle for the Falklands was the successful establishment of the bridgehead at San Carlos. By great good fortune the task force, seven weeks out from Portsmouth and Plymouth and 8,000 miles of ocean from their main base, had managed to get ashore 5,000 men with their heavy weapons, armour, ammunition and stores. Luck is as important to military commanders as it is to gamblers, and they went ashore with little ground force opposition. The Royal Marines and the Parachute Regiment had succeeded in doing something which few armies in the world would attempt to do. With only thin air cover, they had made a successful seaborne landing on the hostile coast of an island known to be defended by an Argentine force estimated at nine or ten thousand strong. Helicopters were also used, but they also were ship-based.

Once a shore base had been established, Brigadier Julian Thompson, Commander of the land force, lost little time in probing forward then launching the 2nd Battalion of the Parachute Regiment on the reinforced defenders of Goose Green and Darwin. There the Paras defeated that force of double their own numbers and took the surrender of no less than 1,400 prisoners. This was the decisive encounter which opened up the way to Stanley.

Because the Royal Navy, despite heavy losses, retained command of the sea and could still fend off the Argentine Air Force, the liner *Queen Elizabeth II* came up and transferred the 5th Infantry Brigade to landing ships. They were then put ashore in conditions of high secrecy. With these reinforcements which brought the British forces up to 8,000, Major General Jeremy Moore, Royal Marines, newly arrived as the

overall land force Commander, was able to lay plans and
make preparations for the final battle. The fighting force at
his disposal was at least as numerous as that of General
Menendez and his defenders. The British objective was clear
and straightforward – to retake the capital and force the
Argentine defenders to surrender.

The British were no longer outnumbered. They had helicopters to reduce the troops' dependence on vehicles and
footslogging. The Commander could by this time make
better use of his meagre resources of Harriers which were
now able to jump off from landing strips at Goose Green and
from the San Carlos bridgehead. General Menendez and his
troops were beleaguered at the narrow end of the island and
at last under a really effective blockade. They were dishear-
tened by news of the surrender at Goose Green and Darwin.

Yet two great worries remained on the mind of the task
force Commander, Rear Admiral Woodward. Despite the
losses it had sustained, estimated at the beginning of June to
be fifty-nine combat aircraft and nine helicopters, the Argentine Air Force still had fighting aircraft in reserve which had
the range and capability to attack the fleet and troops ashore.
The second worry was that Argentina still had a fleet in being
which could not be ignored in the military equation. In
Argentine waters only 300 or 400 miles distant, lurked an
aircraft carrier, two modern destroyers and other less formidable warships. Only once in the earlier stages had the surface
ships shown signs of any desire to approach the British fleet:
when the nuclear-powered submarine HMS *Conqueror* had
sunk the cruiser *General Belgrano* at the approaches to the
exclusion zone. Since that time Royal Navy submarines had
penned in the Argentine fleet in the same style that their
frigate forbears in Nelson's Navy had bottled up Napoleon's
fleet in the Channel ports. But as the military denouement
ashore approached, the Argentine naval Commander still
had three submarines in play which were capable of inflicting
damage.

In principle, Rear Admiral Woodward, with ships pur-
pose-built to withstand submarine attacks by the Soviet

Navy, should have been able to hold off any assault by
Argentine submarines. In other ways the improvised force
was not so well suited to its task. The landing ships and the
troop-carrying liners were protected only by two small aircraft carriers, the venerable *Hermes* and the light anti-
submarine carrier *Invincible*. With an initial force of only two
score of the vertical take-off Sea Harrier and Harrier jets,
they were unable to provide anything like total air cover once
within range of the shore-based air power of Argentina. The
Harriers proved their versatility and attracted the attention
of foreign military onlookers by their performance, but they
had to perform more tasks than they had been designed to
carry out. They flew interception patrols against Mirage and
Skyhawk attack, they attacked and bombed ships and
ground positions, and carried out photographic reconnaissance. But the small packet of Harriers was hard put upon to
be everywhere at once. Military prudence and conventional
wisdom would have dictated that no task force thus equipped
should have even placed itself within three or four hundred
miles of an Air Force as strong as that of Argentina.

   Had this been a war game rather than a real and urgent
military campaign, those who devised it would have insisted
that the British should have at least one big fleet carrier
with squadrons of supersonic interceptor fighters on board.
Ideally they would have been supported by Hawkeye-type
radar flights backed by long range AWACS (Airborne
Warning and Control Systems) to give warning and hold off
land-based squadrons. Such refinements and luxuries of
equipment were not available to Rear Admiral Woodward
and his 25,000 men and women – for by now the force
included nurses, women service personnel and at least one
woman ship's officer. They were not available partly for
sensible reasons of economy in the nation's spending, and
partly because of defence planning calculations about what
the British forces might in future be called upon to do.
Attacking islands in the South Atlantic was not among the
tasks considered.

   Yet at the beginning of April 1982, the fleet *had* to sail on this mission. There was never any doubt in the minds of the government, the Opposition and a large majority of the British people. It amazed the Argentines, it surprised the Americans and the friendly powers of Europe but that is the way it was.

As the task force approached the enemy-occupied shore of the Falklands, the diplomatic alternatives which it was at first planned to back up, ran out with every sea mile covered. But also the military choices were reduced.

There was every sign that Mrs Thatcher's "War Cabinet" in London was determined to keep Admiral Woodward and his officers on a tight leash until the last twitches of international diplomacy had failed. Only then were the services allowed full control to make the landings and win the battles. Other strategic pressures were also at work. Winter was coming on in the south and supply lines were becoming more difficult, especially from Ascension Island onwards. If the islands were to be liberated, then the deed were best done quickly, and storm-tossed troops had to be got ashore. Without air superiority, it would be impossible to achieve an effective sea blockade.

Despite the constant advice not to push things to military action from the alliance of faint-hearts, peace-makers and peace-mongers at home and abroad, Mrs Thatcher and her supporters went ahead. The principal argument for not engaging in war was that lives should at all costs be saved, and dire warnings were delivered about the extent of the bloodshed to be expected.

But the Falklands conflict was a small war and a professional war which reminded historians of those fought in the eighteenth century by limited numbers of full-time soldiers. The British forces were all in this category; so too were the fighting Argentines of the Air Force, Navy and the effective part of the Army which was impeded rather than strengthened by its conscripts. As in earlier small wars, the Falklands one had limited objectives. The only piece of territory which each of the combatant forces wanted to seize, or counter-seize, was the islands, the "heap of rocks". It was far removed in concept from the great peoples' wars, invented by the French Revolution and perfected by Bonaparte, which set the pattern for the murderous slaughter of two World Wars and was echoed later in Vietnam.

In the Falklands battle there was never any question of battalions marching to their doom. Even in the fierce aeronaval engagements, it seemed unlikely that there would be anything like the loss of life comparable to the killing and drowning of the 2,500 men lost when the Royal Navy sank Admiral Graf von Spee's ships off the Falklands in 1914.

This was a small war fought by the limited forces of two countries normally immune from each other's attacks by the facts of geography and equipment which placed them thousands of miles apart. It was a sub-nuclear conflict which could still be contested in high-tech engagements with most of the arsenal of modern technology: missiles, electronics, nuclear-powered submarines, jets and helicopters. Of course men are in charge of the complicated and sophisticated weapons of the eighties, but a good deal of the fighting involves machine fighting machine, missile attacking missile. For this reason, and because comparatively few men are needed on the "weapon platforms" engaged, and although the new weapons are terrible, they tend to take less toll in human life than the older generation military devices of the age of mass production. This is a phenomenon which has been noted in other recent small wars. In 1973, although the Israelis fought long and bitter battles against the Egyptians and Syrians, total casualties were not enormous. Far fewer people were killed in those weeks of conflict than in one forenoon in the Battle of the Somme.

Such military philosophy is, of course, small consolation to those who did die and to those who were bereaved. Even before the final battle, the struggle had cost the lives of 130 British men and 700 Argentines. But these are the unpleasant facts of war which will not be forgotten and from which each side will draw its own conclusions. It remains to be seen whether the Argentines will decide that this was too high a price for the illegal occupation by military force of these offshore islands.

To the surprise of many, Rear Admiral Ramon Asara, adviser to the hawkish Commander of the Argentine Navy, began questioning whether the Falklands were worth the price after the surrender of Goose Green. After publicly referring to "this madness" in which so many lives had been lost, he went on to say: "It is so unfortunate that so many men have died fighting over these islands. I really do not accept that they justify such a cost. Yes, I would say they are not worth fighting for."

A similar, more thoughtful approach was apparent in the words of General Lami Dozo, Commander in Chief of the Argentine Air Force, known for his more democratic views within the junta. His men had fought harder, lost more and won more success than other branches of the armed forces and so his position became more powerful within the triumvirate. Argentina, he said, would have to find a new position for itself in the world for the country had matured since the war started. Before that people were saying that the country needed a war. "Let us see if those who said that will now work for a real Argentina."

Such indications of the way minds were turning in Buenos Aires produced some optimism that once the fighting ceased on the Falklands there might be little enough disposition for the Argentine leadership to fight on by again attacking the British on the Falklands by sea and air. For there were fears in London fostered by the Foreign Office that Britain might be faced with a kind of "South Atlantic Israel" in the Falklands constantly under threat of Argentine revanchism.

On the British side, signs appeared that the cost of the expedition (in terms of lives lost) was hardening the attitude of thinking soldiers engaged in it. Max Hastings, one of the most perceptive of the correspondents on the spot, reported: "I think the only outcome of this war that would cause great bitterness among those who are fighting, is any peace that gives Argentina a share in the Falklands government after we have won."

Even as the fighting continued both Mrs Thatcher's cabinet and British politicians began addressing themselves to the future of the Falkland Islands, and divisions of opinion at once became apparent. Within the inner Cabinet Mr Pym, no doubt influenced by thinking in the Foreign Office over which he presided, was reasserting his earlier statement, "We remain prepared to negotiate with Argentina about the long-term future of the islands." Mrs Thatcher was still convinced that once the Argentine occupiers had been expelled the British Governor should fly back and the Falklands should return to their pre-war position, at least for a long and unspecified period, so that the islanders might recover from their shock and consider what they would like for the future.

The most important consideration is that the small British population of the Falklands must be assured that they can live there without fear of a new attempt to take them over by force. This may well involve some form of international cooperation to guarantee their safety with the participation of the United States, and possibly of Canada and Mexico. Despite that, it will probably be necessary to establish a sizeable British garrison upon the islands which, because of the cost of such an operation, would be reduced as soon as possible.

The question remains whether the islands can be made economically viable without links with Argentina. Already there are plans to develop the islands and encourage investment there. If the Conservative government were persuaded to nationalise the Falkland Islands Company, which owns most of the land there, this might well help in the process. At worst, garrison duty would provide the Army with a useful overseas training ground and its presence would strengthen Britain's claim to a stake in their further development as a base for exploitation of the riches of Antarctica. Useful recommendations already exist in a report drawn up by Lord Shackleton, who is now making a new study.

If port facilities at Stanley were improved, and if an international airport were to be constructed there, the Falklands would become less isolated than in the past. It would all cost money but less than the charge of keeping large forces on the ground, for if a small garrison could be reinforced speedily by air from home bases, the old and proven concept of two frigates and a battalion would be enough to protect the islands from another invasion.

Failure to defend the islands in 1982 brought a war which cost lives and money. But what effect did the conflict have upon international affairs? First it demonstrated the strength of the Western European alliance. NATO gave moral support to Britain. The French and the West Germans showed a high and reassuring degree of loyalty to their sometimes difficult cross-Channel ally. At first the whole European Community, and at some cost to itself, rallied to the cause with unanimity only weakened as the war intensified when the Italians, for understandable reasons, and the Irish for perverse ones, faltered. Yet even after their defection the rest of the Community agreed to prolong sanctions for an indefinite period. It was instructive for those who believe that scars of war never heal to note that West Germany and Japan and Italy for a while all gave support to a country with whom they had been at war within living memory.

Even more importantly the old Anglo-Saxon alliance with the United States held firm, despite the worries of President Reagan that by giving support to Britain he might lose a new friend in Argentina and make more enemies in Latin America. Having tried and failed to reconcile the opponents, he offered his support to Britain. The feeling was always there that he hoped the war would not last too long nor degenerate into "no war, no peace", a state of affairs which would hinder the achievement of American policy aims in Central and South America. The whole of Latin America is understandably of great importance to the US and also a prime target for Soviet penetration.

Yet from the outside it is difficult to see Latin America as a unified continent expressing a general will. It is as full of quarrelling states as Africa. Despite all the sharp words used at the Organisation of American States, not one of the member countries went even so far as to sever diplomatic relations with Britain. So provided the consequences of the Falklands campaign do not linger for too long, it is doubtful whether in the long run the United States will suffer from anything more serious than wordy recrimination.

As the campaign proceeded, there was little sign that the Soviet Union was intent on any serious attempt to win great influence in Argentina. General Lami Dozo declared in June that his country had received no offers of Soviet military aid. When it suited the Kremlin to buy quantities of grain from Argentina, to get round an American partial boycott, it did so. But as soon as grain was available on the North American market and offered more cheaply, the Soviet Union cut back its orders of Argentine grain. This was a decision which may hurt the Argentine economy as much as any sanctions against it which were ordered out of loyalty to Britain. In its dealings with Latin America, the Kremlin remains as cynical as ever ready to exploit situations through propaganda, but support is not forthcoming, even in terms of military equipment, unless it is paid for with hard currency. The Soviets are ideological arms merchants rather than helpful friends of Argentina and they know to their chagrin how great is the cost of their Cuban ally, Fidel Castro.

The attitude of the American public went through a number of changes during the conflict. At first there was amusement at so much fuss over a "heap of rocks" in the Atlantic. This turned to the belief that the dispatch of the task force was just a gesture but horror was expressed at the prospect of a small war which might harm American interests in Latin America. It is always said that generals are usually engaged in fighting again the last war. It is certainly true that many American journalists and media people showed that they were intent upon fighting again the Vietnam war. They expected to see the action on TV being followed inevitably by British repugnance at casualties and by demands for peace. To their surprise none of this came to pass. For reasons of distance from base and strictness of Defence Ministry control, the war was reported on radio and in the papers with little live television coverage, and there was little enough sign that the British would shrink from seeing it through to the end.

What the conflict did do was to demonstrate that, unpleasant though it may be to accept, national quarrels can be settled by fighting, and sometimes they can only be settled by fighting. It can also be argued reasonably that a small war can end in a more satisfactory peace after it has taken place than would have been possible before. So long as neither of the contestants is too severely defeated and humiliated, and each can boast of some victories and acts of courage, peace arrangements can be made. Had it not been for the courageous crossing of the Suez Canal by the Egyptian Army and the fact that it almost defeated the Israelis, it would never have been possible to settle the differences between Egypt and Israel.

In a comparable way the fighting in the South Atlantic succeeded in restoring national pride in Britain, a fact which is likely over the next few years to affect the political and economic life of the country. The same clash had a similar effect upon Argentina, a country which has hitherto never quite succeeded in welding itself into a nation. General Lami Dozo expressed the feeling in grand terms, saying: "We now have a different Argentina which is respected in an international context . . ."

The Falklands Conflict began with the statement that this was a conflict which need never have taken place. If the British had been more prepared it could have been prevented; if the Argentines had not insisted upon invasion there would have been no fighting. Once they did a clash of arms was inevitable. It became a necessary small war. A great deal of rhetoric went into justifying it. Putting all that aside, the simple fact remains that there are times when a democratic state must use military force. It must do so to remind aggressors that, reluctant though countries like Britain are to go to war, it must not be assumed that they will shrink from it when their territory and their rights are threatened.

That is a point worth making for the benefit of nations

more powerful and more dangerous than Argentina who are deluded by the belief that nations of the Western alliance are incapable of fighting to defend their interests. In the words of President Reagan: "We cannot approve of the principle of armed aggression being allowed to succeed."

MORE NON-FICTION FROM CORONET

All these books are available at your local bookshop or newsagent, or can be ordered direct from the publisher. Just tick the titles you want and fill in the form below.

Prices and availability subject to change without notice.

CORONET BOOKS, P.O. Box 11, Falmouth, Cornwall.

Please send cheque or postal order, and allow the following for postage and packing:

U.K. – 45p for one book, plus 20p for the second book, and 14p for each additional book ordered up to a £1.63 maximum.

B.F.P.O. and EIRE – 45p for the first book, plus 20p for the second book, and 14p per copy for the next 7 books, 8p per book thereafter.

OTHER OVERSEAS CUSTOMERS – 75p for the first book, plus 21p per copy for each additional book.

Name ....

Address ....

....